Getting On, Falling Off

From adoption and finding life and love in the Far East to fighting a losing battle with Parkinson's Disease

BY MICHAEL BROADBENT

www.pearlescapes.co.uk

pearl@pearlescapes.co.uk

Distributed in the UK by

Flying Machine Films Ltd.

Chichester Enterprise Centre, Terminus Rd, Chichester

West Sussex, PO19 8TX, United Kingdom

For Joyce

Contents

About the Author

'If you can meet with Triumph and Disaster
And treat those two impostors just the same;'
Rudyard Kipling, *If-*

Mike Broadbent was born in Oxford in 1954 to an ill-fated couple who were not able to bring him up. He was swiftly adopted by a loving and caring Yorkshire family.

From then on Mike's family life, schooling and university education were entirely appropriate for a middle class child of the time, although always shaped on his part by an incredible drive and work ethic. This trait was accentuated and focused by Sedbergh School, which had a formative influence on him including instilling a fierce sense of competition. There he acquired a love of rugby and English literature both of which were lifelong passions. He thrived at Cambridge University reading English. He coupled academic brilliance with a colossal appetite for work, which resulted in a Double First and the highest awards for his achievements. He was the best that Cambridge could produce, but even he discovered the difficulties of 'What next?'

He found the answer in Hong Kong with a career-defining role as head of public relations at HSBC. It was a time of massive flux for HSBC and Hong Kong. He helped transition the bank to London and communicate the changes in business that the 1997 handover to China would bring. He rose to every professional challenge and opportunity again harnessing his Herculean capacity for work. However he still found time, somehow, to travel and see the world, and meet the love of his life – Joyce Chiu.

He was a victim of his own success and was asked by HSBC to return to London. Although desperately sad to leave his beloved Hong Kong, he prepared to take on an exciting new chapter as head of the HSBC Group Corporate Affairs Department, a massive global responsibility.

However, all future plans were catastrophically upended by a diagnosis of early onset Parkinson's Disease. He now faced the biggest challenge of his life. Described as incurable, but not terminal, PD, as he and Joyce came to call it, dominated the last chapters of his life, but could not prevent his determination to exercise his independence, discover the truth about his birth, participate in difficult medical trials and to write this book.

In the last five years of his life, he found it a challenge to make himself understood because his speech was so slurred, and he had to type with one finger. His life had shaped him to rise above every difficulty and nowhere was this better demonstrated than by the way he took on the last years of his life. He never once lapsed into self-pity, but met PD with every strength he had, aided by Joyce who was at his side throughout and a constant source of care, concern and comfort.

Throughout all his suffering, his unquenchable and supreme sense of wit and humour shone through. Mike's book was first published privately for friends and family in 2018. In the same year Joyce published her companion book of poetry, *From The Heart*. Both books sat under the Christmas tree that year, the third Christmas they shared since doctors had told them to expect no more. Mike Broadbent died on February 21st, 2019.

Acknowledgements

I am particularly grateful to Stephen Green, former Group Chairman of HSBC and an author of distinction, for encouraging me to start writing and to keep going when it became physically difficult to do so. I am also profoundly grateful to Edwin Green, formerly a respected colleague, and for a long time a dear friend, for his expertise in polishing an error-strewn and bituminous manuscript. Thanks are also due to Hilary Green for bringing her own considerable editing skills to bear on a project which offered no obvious gain, and for her resourceful sleuthing, along with Chris Bale, shining a light on a subject which had long been buried.

From Joyce

While I share Mike's sentiments, I would also like to express my heartfelt gratitude to those who helped with this second edition of Mike's memoir:

To David Beaves, a dear friend of Mike, for his contribution to the About the Author section. It was never going to be easy to write. His kind and insightful words about Mike touched me.

To Libby Chiu, my sister, who wrote the Foreword. She said things about Mike and my life with him that I could not.

To Richard Bennett and David Shaw, former colleagues of Mike, for their wise legal counsel in the context of the chapter on Hong Kong.

To Carol Benson, my best friend, whose profession as a teacher helped cast a beady eye on any typing and grammatical mistakes.

To Pearl Howie, my editor and publisher, who made it possible for Mike's private memoir to reach a wider audience.

Preface

This publication has not been commissioned by any organisation.

The narrative is the honest view of the author at the time of writing, before his death on February 21st 2019.

He would have been sad to learn of the violent events in Hong Kong in 2019, at the time the second edition of this book is being published.

Foreword

Written by Libby Chiu

When a man of honour passes away, we mourn his loss, and we celebrate his enduring legacy. Mike Broadbent was such a man, and I will always value him as my brother-in-law, married to my sister Joyce, and as a friend. My husband Peter and I had the privilege of attending their wedding in 1990, and their renewal of their wedding vows thirteen years later. At these momentous events, and in so many everyday moments, we witnessed Mike's deep love for Joyce. As Joyce's protective older sister, I, needless to say, kept an eagle eye on him, and so noticed Mike's quiet gaze of love and wonderment at his wife. I found, among Mike's many admirable qualities, one that really moved me was his respect for Joyce's devotion to nurturing her spirituality, and leading a mindful life. Mike's quiet strength and the subtle expression of his innermost emotions demonstrated that intangible beauty of a strong marriage, one that embodies the grace of unity – two temperaments, one soul of love.

We all admired Mike's towering intellect, and we were charmed by his humility. He could propose a thesis that would connect the Fall of the Roman Empire to the Meiji Restoration, even while hoisting a beer at the local pub overlooking the Yorkshire Dales. Worlds far apart, but in one world created for us by Mike.

Mike had a sly love of whimsy that was simply delightful. I shudder to think what Mike would have thought of that observation. I, and others, have often thought that, were Mike not a banker, he would have made a formidable interrogator, oft throwing the proverbial curve ball of seemingly random questions. On his first visit to Peter and me in the United States, he asked about the demographics of Boston where we were living, amongst other queries. I was nonplussed, and had not an answer; Mike was quite pleased with himself.

When he next visited, he asked, "When is sunset tonight?"

I replied, "8:17pm."

I received the rare reward of a sheepish grin from Mike. Joyce applauded merrily, and I was most proud of myself at that moment.

There were instances of utter amusement from Mike, for example, at Joyce's rules of domestic order. Once, he wryly told me that I should not sit still for too long, as Joycie, his pet name for my sister, would likely fold me up and pack me into a drawer.

Parkinson's Disease brought on physical struggles, but Mike maintained his humanity. On one of our last visits to London to see Mike, he valiantly took Peter to the Imperial War Museums to honour Peter's long-time desire to see Sir Winston Churchill's War Rooms. We are forever grateful for Mike's fundamental thoughtfulness.

During our last visit to the Lake District, a robin flew to Joyce, perched itself on a rock, and sang sweetly and directly to her. We all gathered behind Joyce, and listened. May the robin's trill forever keep Mike's voice in Joyce's heart.

"All is well
All is well
With my soul."

Prologue

'The history of the world is but the biography of great men.'

Thomas Carlyle, *Heroes and Hero-worship*

'Discuss.'

Carlyle's famous dictum frequently appears in undergraduate and A level examination papers. At least it used to. So, let me stress from the outset that this account of my life is not based on any delusions that anything I ever did remotely resembles the achievements of men and women whose lives will be remembered 100 years from now – the statesmen, generals, scientists who made an indelible mark on the world and the writers and artists whose work speaks down the ages. They are the men and women deserving of biographies. I was merely an attendant lord, one who would do to swell a progress, start a scene or two.

In fact, I wrote this book for my own benefit in a cathartic effort to make sense of my life, when after some years of comparative success and good fortune, things took a radical turn for the worse, sooner than is normal. Secondly, I wanted to leave a record of my profound gratitude to my wonderful wife, Joyce, and to an outstanding group of friends who have remained loyal and supportive through thick and thin. There is little reason why an account of an otherwise unremarkable life should appeal to a wider audience. However, should the book happen to enter the public domain, it may be of passing interest to those, either parents or children, who have experience of adoption, or to those who are suffering from long-term, incurable illness. It is just plausible that the two are connected. In different ways they can affect deeply the direction of a human life and there is comfort in shared experience. Happily, on the one hand, and sadly on the other, I can claim some knowledge of both.

One point of style; I make frequent use of literary references. These may not mean much to the reader. If they do, they will hopefully illustrate or amplify the point I am trying to make by enlisting the support of the best that has been thought or said on a subject. If they appear baffling or simply pretentious, I apologise; it is a reflection of the way I think, and the vast number of hours I spent at Cambridge assimilating all this stuff.

Chapter 1 - The Background

'We will now discuss in a little more detail the struggle for existence.' Charles Darwin, *The Origin of the Species*

I was born in the Radcliffe Infirmary, on Walton Street, Oxford, in the early hours of 3 May 1954. I was told by someone who was there that it was an uncomplicated birth. The only remarkable thing about it was that my mother was 150 miles away at the time.

The woman who bore me was called Catherine Alice Tooley, except that was not her legal name and nor, in those days when such things still counted for something, was she married to my natural father or, for that matter, to anyone else. She remembers vividly the moment I emerged into the world – slightly breathless but uncomplaining. But then she also remembers, with savage clarity, the next moment. Not for her the transcendent joy that is nature's lavish reward for the pain of childbirth, nor the moment when, for the first time, a mother takes her new son or daughter into her arms. She remembers – a void. She says (and despite her self-control the grief is just below the surface) she caught the merest glimpse of her son before a stern looking nurse took the boy in her arms, quickly, and deliberately turned her back on Catherine and marched out of the room.

That was the last she was to see or hear of me for the next thirty-five years. An immense sadness settled on her and never lifted. She told me once that, in a life full of bad experiences, this was by some distance the worst. She said that if she lived to be 100 (which she very nearly did) nothing could hurt as much, be more permanently heartbreaking, nor leave such deep emotional scars as that climactic act of separation. It defined her life because at that moment part of Catherine died. She issued a silent howl of anguish as someone slipped a needle into her arm and when she awoke, hours later, part of her soul had shut down.

Someday, well into the future, in a time of greater understanding, experts would refer to this trauma as the 'primal wound' and would claim to understand the profound effects of separation on mothers and on children. But all Catherine knew as she walked out of the hospital two days later was that she could never be happy again. And she was right.

It is July 1988 and I am sitting in the tiny living room of Catherine's flat in South London, where I have gone to meet her for the first time. Or should that be the second? I would like to get to know her a little, to have the opportunity at least to

22

form a first impression of her and to hear what she has to say. I have prepared in my head a few routine questions to put to her, such as who am I, where did I come from, why did you abandon me, what characteristics or talents (if any) am I likely to display and what diseases are likely to form part of my genetic inheritance? How long am I likely to live? Not long at the current rate, I say to myself, because I am sitting there chain smoking, having eaten little of the food which I can see she has been to great trouble to prepare.

So far it has been an awkward meeting, stilted conversation interspersed with uncomfortable silences. As usual I retreat into my reading. Is this the way to play Samuel Beckett I ask myself? *'Orphan'* – a play for two characters sitting at opposite sides of the stage. Catherine is an elegantly dressed woman (the director insists on this). She looks slightly out of place in her own home, in the most ordinary surroundings. On the other side, the reserved, casually dressed man who looks anything but casual in manner and who is used to meetings in rather more opulent settings. They have a bond, yet they are complete strangers. They share at least one characteristic – a chronic reticence that makes conversation difficult, even though there is so much to say. Their reserve fills the room like a November fog, chilling the air. Neither of them has the strength of character, or the courage, or the recklessness, or whatever it takes to cut through it. Nature may have created them mother and son. But there is no sign that an umbilical chord ever joined them. And there has been no gushing, tearful reunion, no collapsing into each other's arms crying, 'At last, at last.'

Actually, I never expected there would be. Not after so many years and not with people like us. For all the shows of bonhomie and a genuine affection for family and friends, we have revealed little of ourselves to the outside. People like us are intensely private. We keep ourselves to ourselves, living lives of what James Joyce called 'silence, exile and cunning'.

I have to say, however, that even I have been a little taken aback by the business-like way she has ushered me into her home. Imagining the moment while sitting in an empty train compartment on my way to Sutton to meet Catherine, I had indulged in a little harmless daydreaming. I had allowed for a wide-eyed stare of incredulity or a gasp of surprise and pleasure that a lifelong wish had been granted. There was neither.

Instead, I felt like a visiting tradesman, invited with cold politeness to stay for a cup of tea, accepting out of politeness and then quickly regretting his decision.

So far, only one, very strange, thing has happened. When she first opens the door to me and I see this elderly, dignified woman who has played no part in my life except to create it, I feel strong sexual attraction. Just for a second or two. Then it vanishes.

How on earth could I react to her like that? For God's sake, she is old enough to be your... I feel deeply ashamed. Then my mind selects the right file. Of course. Freud and Oedipus, I doff my cap to you, sage of Vienna.

Anyway, after a moment's hesitation she invites me in and it couldn't be more prosaic. I feel like a plumber summoned to fix a leaking radiator and the hint of weary resignation in her voice suggests it must have been the second or third time she had called me out in a fortnight. I had considered making a witty remark by way of an opening; something to break the ice and put us at our ease, something like, 'Hello Mum, sorry I'm late. I just went out to get some milk.' I had discarded the idea almost immediately. It would trivialise what might be the critical moment of her life. Like a crude and tasteless best man's speech at a wedding, it could ruin her day. At worst it could be profoundly distressing and offensive. In any case there was no ice to break; we had not even reached the water's edge.

And right now, when my mind is blank and I am tongue tied and trying to think of something to say that would fill the silence, I wish I had prepared a proper list of the questions that I had mused on, and forgotten, while on the train. This might have helped us along and perhaps enabled me to stay in control of the conversation. I even wonder if I should have given her notice of them in advance. She is your mother for God's sake, not an Opposition MP.

Some homecoming, I say to myself.

Is she really like this or is it a protective carapace designed to shield her from the world and the enormity of the occasion? It's not clear.

I make a brief opening speech before we sit down to eat but I rush it due to nerves. The words pour out in a torrent and I fluff my lines badly. I try to explain that I have come in peace, seeking only the truth. I do not wish to reproach, not to accuse, not to judge but to try simply to understand. I say that I have wonderful adoptive parents, that life has been good to me, that I have had every possible opportunity to make something of myself, that I have taken them gratefully, making the most of such abilities that I possess. In other words, I am getting on with life and doing quite nicely thank you. But then I go off on some ridiculous tangent about Hong Kong. And I am burbling about the Sino-British Joint Declaration on the future of Hong Kong and Catherine is looking baffled before I realise how far I have strayed off-piste from my theme.

So, I try to get back with one of those unsound bridging sentences, 'As I was saying…' (which I wasn't) and I assure Catherine that I am neither angry nor bitter, and that I am sure she did the right thing in the circumstances (whatever they were) – and here she interjects with confidence, 'an absolute necessity,' and that she should never feel guilty or reproach herself (even if she doesn't). But it all comes across as insincere and over rehearsed (which it certainly isn't).

I now turn my assessment 180 degrees, towards myself. I judge it a pity that I could not simply have extemporised because, although I don't say a lot, when I do speak it is normally thoughtful and in complete sentences. In fact, I am usually an articulate man with a keen sense of 'le mot juste'. That is my job after all, and that would have sounded more natural and more honest. Instead, we have neither fish nor fowl. I offer neither the hint of preparation nor the trace of the spontaneity the occasion demands. I stand in the middle of her tiny flat delivering a formal speech that makes me sound like a senior civil servant giving the address at his old school prize giving. What a mess.

Now I am looking for the opportunity to try again but the trail has gone cold.

We sit like an ill matched pair of Quakers, waiting for the spirit to move us. It is taking a hell of a long time. I begin to wonder if I have done the right thing in coming here. I must have disturbed ghosts long since laid to rest. And for what purpose, to what end? Past is past except that, as Ibsen knew, it is never completely silent.

I am about to leave, having apologised for coming back from her past to trouble her. There is an unbridgeable gap between us; the silence is oppressive and part of my mind is shrieking, 'For God's sake, let's get out of here. This is just too awkward.' But I persevere, telling myself you made a big effort to reach this point; don't waste it. And Catherine, you too have waited a long time and you have to confront your past. If you have ever felt guilty about giving me up, about abandoning me, this is the time for your redemption. You are so formal, so sardonic that it is hard to grasp what you would have been without the huge burden you have carried, without the dead weight of a conscience that has pressed down on you for almost forty years. After all, most people would agree that it is no small thing to give up a child... wouldn't they?

I resolve to stay, at least for a few more minutes.

I light another cigarette and settle back in my chair.

And I try to jump-start the conversation yet again. I ask Catherine to tell me about her own parents and childhood and feel immediately that this is the right angle from which to approach an appallingly difficult subject. This is encouraging; I now feel more like George Smiley, gently but ruthlessly interrogating Connie Sachs, getting her to dredge her extraordinary memory for the one piece of information that will lead him to Karla. And who or what is my Karla? Good question.

Suddenly, as if sensing that the ice is now safe to walk on, Catherine tiptoes forward and begins to speak in a barely audible whisper that becomes louder as she grows in confidence.

Taking great care not to interrupt her and make her lose momentum I nod in silent encouragement and I listen as profoundly as I can.

And now, like a child learning to ride a bicycle, Catherine has found her balance, and is up and pedalling and this is what I have come half way round the world to hear. At last, after an hour of absurd trivia, Catherine is telling me her story. This is her confession, bottled up inside her, shared with no one – no one – for four decades. The floodgates open and her whole terrible story gushes out.

It is not a particularly exciting or dramatic story. In fact, it is commonplace. But it is her story and so it is mine and it is worth hearing for the first time. It speaks of events that must have happened thousands of times and to many thousands of people. It is a story about the tragedy of everyday life. Catherine tells it calmly, coolly, almost dispassionately as though she is describing the life of someone else, someone she once knew but not well. Not a close friend. Not an intimate. Yet it is the saddest personal story I have ever heard. And she is the saddest person I have ever met. She talks without a trace of self-pity, a brief, sardonic laugh the only betrayal of her emotions which otherwise are in held firmly in check.

'Things were very different in those days,' she intones.

I approve. It is a good, smooth entry into her narrative, reminding me a little of a story by Joseph Conrad.

Catherine is a good storyteller. She is interesting and funny and deeply, profoundly sad. Today, she tells only the outline of the story; bear in mind that it is a first meeting and enough is enough.

We shall meet only twice more but, in the months ahead, she will write voluminous letters filling in the details from an impressive memory.

I will send short, increasingly impersonal replies.

Years later, I will conclude that she actually prefers writing to meeting. She is highly literate and I think that she feels more comfortable writing than talking face to face with a complete stranger, who is her son. I think my physical presence intrudes on her own little world. She knows it is far too late to reclaim me; I am not an item of lost luggage.

Nevertheless, today is hugely important and once she gets going it is hard to interrupt the flow. She is amusing and very sad. The light moments underline the bad. She understands this instinctively. In life as in art and literature, the author knows how to control the tempo in order to inflict the greatest pain on his audience. It is how Shakespeare controls the momentum of the great tragedies with scenes of comedy; the Porter in *Macbeth*; the gravedigger in *Hamlet*, the Fool in *King Lear*. The audience needs a breather before the wheels of the rack on which their emotions are stretched are turned once more. That's the way to build pressure.

Also, there is the question of perspective. Tolstoy said that there are few more agreeable experiences than to look back on a time of great unhappiness while enjoying a period of happiness and that the converse is also true. Catherine's story is told from the perspective of the unhappy on the even more unhappy, but she describes the bad with a degree of black humour and the good with a touch of lightness. Most of her narration, however, is in a voice of flat detachment. It is short of major contrasts and perhaps it is not so immediately moving because of that. It is flat, drab and grey. It is the tone of the weary and the defeated.

Although she is clearly intelligent and self-aware she seems to me to lack the emotional or moral stature of the classical tragic hero or heroine. But, come to think of it, so do I. She is no Tess of the D'Urbervilles surrounded by blood red symbols, which mark her as an Aeschylean heroine. There are no brilliant whites of the kind we associate with the Duchess of Malfi ('Cover her face, mine eyes dazzle, she died young').

Catherine seems to have been singled out by the Gods for special treatment. She is, in a very real sense in a different

31

category; she is quite exceptionally ordinary. Usually one can follow the complex interplay of how character and circumstance can conspire to bring about the downfall of the victim. Or if the linkage is not immediately apparent, trying out different grips on the hinge that leads to disaster will ultimately reveal the fatal flaw. However, Catherine is not a bad person; she does nothing particularly wrong. At worst, she suffers from a fatal acquiescence, a docility that prevents her from fighting and from swimming hard against the tide of misfortune that comes her way. She is too weak to resist the tragic circumstances that lie in her path, but too strong to let them destroy her. Accordingly, she is condemned to spend most of her time on earth suspended between the pull of misfortune and the push of her awareness of what her life could have been. In the classical sense of the word she is not tragic at all, but in the extent of her suffering she has few peers. In my darker moments I wonder how much I inherited and how much I resemble her, if at all.

Chapter 2 - Catherine's Story

Catherine was born in Kent in 1917. It was, to say the least, an inauspicious year. The Great War, the war to end all wars, was in its fourth year and had become a futile stalemate. America had at last entered on the side of the Allies and had sent a large number of troops and a massive amount of materiel to Europe but, except for their demoralising influence on German public opinion, had yet to make a significant impact on the course of the war.

The casualties on both sides were colossal and in the early autumn came the battle that became the culminating symbol of the entire conflict and, in a way, of all wars.

The allies launched yet another offensive into the Ypres salient. But heavy rain for weeks on end turned the battlefield into a quagmire. For the sake of a few miles gained, thousands of men died; someone would later calculate the cost at 400 dead per square metre, many of them not even killed by enemy fire but drowning in the mud. It was an attempted advance that should never have been attempted in such conditions.

Third Ypres, Passchendaele, has been called the most horrific battle in human history. 'Dulce et decorum est pro patria mori' famously wrote Wilfred Owen, with heavy irony.

Or as one wag put it, 'All that mud, blood and endless poetry.'

Amongst the two million allied troops deployed on the western front that year was a twenty-one year old second lieutenant with the Royal Irish Rifles. He had lied about his age to enter Kitchener's army and had already accumulated five years of service, including almost three years of continuous fighting.

At a time when the life expectancy of second lieutenants on some parts of the line was measured in weeks rather than months or years he was very much alive, and finding the war almost enjoyable. The high casualty rates made room for fast promotion and the army did not care about the calamitous family life he had left behind. It gave him the opportunity to make a fresh start and to create a new identity.

His real name was Fred Simmons Tooley, although for some reason that I have never discovered, everyone called him Jack.

He survived the Great War and the Second World War and lived long enough to father a son at the age of 58.

By the following year the German public, if not the German army, had had enough and the First World War limped to its interim conclusion (to be continued at a later date).

However, Europe's travails were far from over. Peace brought not only punitive terms for Germany; it also brought a plague of Biblical proportions. It was as if God was punishing mankind for its chronic inability to live in harmony with itself and nature. The great Spanish 'flu epidemic of 1918-20 killed more people than the War itself.

Amongst more than 20 million dead were both Catherine's parents. At the age of eighteen months her life had already taken a blow from which it would never recover. Whether it was sheer bad luck or divine intervention she would never know. Her descent into hell had started.

Her parents had belonged to Kent's solid and respectable middle class and had a thriving business. Many years later she was told by someone who had known them, that they were good, kind people. She had no reason to doubt it. Had they survived she would have had a reasonable expectation of a full education (they believed that clever girls should go to university), a good marriage to a man with a profession, children, a comfortable lifestyle and a place in the community. Even now, after all she has been through, one can imagine her as a leading light in the Women's Institute while her husband, a keen Rotarian (and, sotto voce, a prominent Freemason) also does good works. Together they make an admirable contribution to their community and when they die the church is full for both their funerals, and the vicar, a friend for years, leads the congregation with real feeling. He exhorts his flock to be grateful that Catherine and her husband of 56 years lived amongst them and not sad they have departed. They will always be remembered for the work they did for the poor. The poor... The irony is savage.

Instead, the defenceless infant, cast adrift by misfortune, was taken in, very reluctantly and only after financial inducement, by a childless uncle and aunt, embittered because they had not attained the social status of her parents. They neither loved nor wanted her. If they did not abuse her physically (she was vague on this point) they certainly did so verbally and emotionally. They took revenge on Catherine for their own crippled lives. For eighteen years the only personal or family relationship she knew was a wall of seething, silent resentment.

Catherine's one consolation during this period was her school. Here she was able to look at herself in a full-length mirror, rather than the distorted prism of her hateful foster parents. She discovered that she was bright, witty and articulate. She also realised as she entered her teens that despite the thick face of reserve that she showed to the outside world, she was popular. Although no one could get close enough to her to form a deep friendship, she was well liked. She was teased, but also respected for the puritanical correctness she displayed in her dealings with her fellow pupils. People trusted her because she was utterly trustworthy. And discreet. And loyal. Although the state of her clothes spoke of poverty (her guardians were as miserly with their allowance as they were with their affection) she did not suffer the taunting which children, with their capacity for collective cruelty, often inflict on the outsider or the member of the tribe who cannot keep up. Tall for her age and possessed of a quiet dignity that discouraged bullying, Catherine did well at school. And since there was obviously no prospect of her going to university, on the day she left school she also left home, the latter without a backward glance.

She wrote a polite note which she placed under a cup on the kitchen table thanking her uncle and aunt for stepping into the breach left by her parents, apologising for having inconvenienced them and assuring them that she would not trouble them further. It is doubtful that they grasped the irony. Catherine was as good as her word. She never contacted them again.

And so, innocent, inexperienced, without close friends, money or even the outline of a plan but with a reasonable education, a good practical mind and stout heart she went out into the world. At the age of eighteen she should probably have been anxious about what to do next but she was not. Instead she was suffused with an enormous sense of relief that she was at last escaping that detested little corner of Kent. She determined to put as much distance as possible between herself and her childhood.

She took the train from Canterbury to London. She tried to look for work there but she found the city overwhelmingly noisy and frenetic for her taste and so she soon headed west following the Thames, staying briefly in Henley and Marlow until she found herself in a part of Oxfordshire which she liked.

In a village just outside Abingdon she found a job working in a hotel. The work, part cleaner, part waitress, was menial but the manager, disabled from injuries sustained in the Great War, was kind, the other members of staff were friendly and most of the customers were agreeable. And best of all, although the pay was poor, the job came with a room in a small but pretty cottage that she shared with three other girls. The visitor to the town can still see it, a half-timbered house just off the main street. It has been beautifully maintained. If it were ever put up for sale it would be described as 'bijou' by the estate agents and would probably be snapped up for a distinctly non-bijou price as a weekend retreat by a young investment banker. However, it is still owned by the hotel and is still occupied by the female staff who work there. They do not do things in a hurry in Abingdon.

Externally, the house looks exactly the same. Inside it has been modernised with the installation of a new kitchen and the luxury of a central heating system.

Many girls have lived here since Catherine's day, and it has an unmistakably feminine air about it. Since many of the temporary staff now come from overseas there are little souvenirs everywhere; from the Netherlands and Germany, Croatia and Poland, Australia and New Zealand. None of them would have matched Catherine's rare smile of delight as she opened the front door for the first time. Also, the profile of the girls has changed a little and it is possible that Catherine would have had more in common with the university graduates from Auckland, Melbourne, Krakow and Berlin, who make up most of the hotel's current complement of casual workers, rather than girls who were to be her colleagues and housemates of the 1930s; most of these came from nearby farms and the poorer areas of Oxford, such as Cowley. Nevertheless, Catherine was no snob either intellectually or socially and she knew as soon as she saw the cottage that it would be just right for her.

She emerged as the natural leader of the four. They were unsophisticated and uneducated and required a certain amount of house training. The manager noted with approval the immediate effect 'the new lass from Kent', as he referred to her, had on their performance. He made it a rule that before any new girl could be let loose on the customers she should undergo coaching by Catherine who appeared to have a natural flair and elegance.

In this way Catherine established herself as an important member of staff at the hotel and as a well liked, albeit reticent, member of the village's small, inward-looking community.

From time to time she talked to the owner about needing to move on but she could never tell him where or to what or why she needed to move. And she always relented, for Catherine was no Emma Bovary, in search of romance and the glamourous life of the city while living in the prosaic reality of the countryside. He always persuaded her to stay, with a mixture of modest pay increases, generous praise and stern lectures about how the grass was not always greener. And she had to admit that the arrangement suited her quite well.

She was not completely devoid of ambition and knew that intellectually she was capable of taking on more demanding work; yet something held her back and somehow she never got round to doing anything about it. At times she suffered from depression and she did not know what caused it but in the safety of the hotel and the cottage she managed to mask it.

Catherine stayed in the village for several more months and then several more and the months turned into years. Although she recognised the passing of the seasons and the power of the sun, the darkness of her childhood cast a shadow across her soul. Inside her mind it was always winter and the thaw never came.

With the passing of time, people came and went and the composition of the cottage changed and changed again. Yet it was almost always a happy and harmonious house, even when, in the busy summer months, the hotel took on extra staff and there were five or six staying in the cottage in impossibly cramped conditions. The cottage, and indeed much of the running of the hotel, was presided over by Catherine, unelected and unofficial but increasingly influential. The other girls looked to her for advice and more often than not they took it.

Catherine was equally popular with the customers whom she served three days a week behind the bar. They were a mixture; local farmers, retirees, executives from the Morris works at Cowley sometimes alone, sometimes taking their wives (sometimes their mistresses), occasionally a quietly flowing don from the university, for lunch and a drive in the country. On a lively evening when the atmosphere was conducive she would join in the banter. The customers found her charming, interesting, witty and surprisingly well read. Everyone liked her but no one could get to know her well. She deflected all personal questions, especially those about her past with a sardonic humour that became her trademark, and she remained an intensely private person. Several times, a regular customer thinking he had got to know her and sensing that they were getting on well, would ask her out. This was predictable given that she was tall, slim, attractive and evidently unattached. She always declined their invitations but usually managed to do so without giving offence, whereupon they would turn their attentions to the other girls who sometimes did accept their invitations.

On one occasion a middle-aged man whose suggestion of a lunch or a dinner or 'a spin in his new Alvis' had been declined, asked for her permission to approach one of her young colleagues. He wanted to know if the speed with which he proposed to change allegiance would hurt her feelings.

'Not in the least,' came the slightly haughty reply and he left the hotel looking crushed.

The only problem with Catherine, observed the regulars, several of whom admired her, was that she seemed so damn self-contained. There was clearly nothing wrong with them – they had cars and they had money – but she was impressed by neither and nor did she appear to have any desire for material things nor any need of emotional attachment. She was self-possessed, an enigma. It prompted at least one of them to ask if Catherine was hiding something through the exercise of steely self-control; at least that would be preferable to the thought that she was simply devoid of normal emotions.

Her colleagues talked about it in idle moments but none guessed the effects on the human psyche of spending eighteen formative years in an utterly loveless world. And what did it matter since she was a pleasant, even-tempered person who was hard working, resolutely cheerful and highly competent? In any case, people would soon have something else to think about.

Catherine was 22 when the Second World War broke out. Still working at the hotel, still unattached, still popular and still a closed book.

The manager asked her what she proposed to do now that the country was at war. He had expected her to say she was leaving to join the WRENS, the WRACS or some other part of the services. Wounded in 1916 and invalided out of the army with both legs badly broken, he was a patriotic soldier who expected that everyone would rush to do their duty. However, if he expected Catherine to say that she had already joined the SOE and was waiting to be parachuted into occupied France with a dagger between her teeth, he was sadly mistaken.

To his direct question what did she plan to do to overthrow Hitler, he received a direct answer; 'Nothing.'

Thinking she must have misheard him, he tried again, 'Nothing,' was the answer.

Closer questioning revealed that she was not a conscientious objector, nor ruled out of service by a hidden disability. She simply wasn't interested in the war or its outcome and not remotely influenced by the populist rhetoric. She was an outsider.

He must have swallowed hard before continuing the discussion but in the end he gave in; Catherine was implacably opposed to change and it was tempting to keep a long serving and experienced member of his staff when he could see that there was going to be a demand for able bodied people from every sector. Besides, he had grown quite fond of her himself.

So, Catherine spent the war years in a pleasant village in Oxfordshire, her conscience untroubled by a higher calling.

In September 1941 she saw on the front page of the newspaper, delivered every morning, a detailed report that the town in Kent where she had been born and neglected had been badly bombed three nights in a row. She simply noted the article and carried on with her work. She made no attempt to discover if her foster parents had survived the attack.

When I first learned of Catherine's detached attitude to the War I felt disappointed in her. I would have been overjoyed had she been an ambulance driver, a fire warden or a nurse. That's when I realised the extent to which I had been assimilated into the Broadbent family and inculcated with its values. The Broadbents, my adoptive family, queued up to do their national service; Catherine had little sense of civic duty and why should she?

She had been virtually abandoned; civil society meant little to her. She was an outsider and always would be. Her foster parents were responsible for her alienation, setting a

44

shining example in selfishness and small-minded cruelty. She had grown up in an atmosphere of glacial resentment. The word 'adopted' was used as a threat held over her like a Damocletian sword. The inference was always that she was surplus to requirements, a cost to be cut, a saving to be made. 'Adopted', her foster parents could make whatever they chose of that label and they chose to make a stick to beat her with. She was merely repaying the favour.

If Catherine's attitude to the War was morally ambiguous, materially it was relatively privileged for someone in her humble station in life. The official supplies of food to the hotel, paltry and unappetising as they were, were supplemented generously, if illegally, by the entrepreneurial flair of local farmers who participated with enthusiasm in the nation's thriving black market, which was far larger than the Government ever realised. Well-to-do farmers visiting the hotel with their families for Sunday lunch might well compliment Catherine and the staff for the quality of the lamb, pork, chicken and vegetables served to them; much of the food they had eaten came from their farms.

It was all very well for Mr Churchill to offer nothing but blood, toil, tears and sweat but he looked well fed, and rumour had it that the cigars and brandy he consumed were imported from America just for him.

And it was fine for the Government to put up posters appealing to the public to 'Eat less bread' in a drive to reduce the amount of wheat that must be transported by the perilous Atlantic convoys. How else was one supposed to consume the huge mound of butter that had been brought through the kitchen door that morning before being served with fresh bread by pretty waitresses in black skirts and white blouses?

It was surprising that such flagrant mutual back scratching did not attract the attention of the rationing authorities in the area. However, the absence of a whistle-blower was testament to the fierce determination of the people of a rural community to get through the War together and with as little discomfort as possible. Their relaxed attitude was helped by the almost complete absence of bombing in the area. This was surprising given that Oxford was within range and was home to the huge Morris plant (now converted to full time production of Spitfires and Hurricanes). The locals said that Hitler favoured Oxford because it was a communications hub in case of invasion and there was even a rumour that he had identified Blenheim Palace as the headquarters of a Nazi-controlled Britain.

Blissfully unconcerned about who governed Britain, Catherine was in the hotel restaurant late one morning just after the war ended. As usual she was tidying up the bar. The room

46

was empty and it was about twenty minutes before opening time. She looked up from the shelves she was cleaning to see a man standing at the entrance.

He was of medium height but powerfully built and looked to be in his mid to late forties. His hair was dark brown but flecked with grey and cut short. His spotless black shoes, military moustache and ill-fitting blue demob suit, that was far too tight for his broad shoulders, left her in no doubt that he was an ex-serviceman.

'Good morning,' he said, 'would I be too early to get a drink?'

Possibly Irish, she thought but could not place him with certainty.

As he approached the bar, Catherine saw that he walked with a limp, but despite this he marched briskly toward her and his hard, rather forbidding look was transformed by a smile into a kinder, gentler, expression. Catherine thought him rather handsome for his age and also sad. She heard herself say, as if from a distance, 'Well, it is a little early but I dare say that an exception could be made for a returning hero.'

'I'm no hero; just the office boy,' he replied.

And as she said later with customary dryness, 'It was a classic case of eyes across an empty room.'

He told her that he had arrived in the area recently and was looking for work. He said his name was Jack Tooley, and when she asked him what his skills were, he said he had been a soldier for most of his adult life but could turn his hand to almost anything.

She told him that as far as she knew there were no openings at the hotel and suggested that he try the Post Office where job advertisements were placed.

He thanked her, stayed until shortly after the official opening time, finished his drink, and left.

The following evening, he returned, bought a drink, offered to buy her one (she declined) and then, according to Catherine's satirical account (she cannot help herself), he took up a position on a stool at one end of the bar and did not leave it for three weeks. He chatted amiably to anyone who came into the bar and, when she was working there and it was not busy, he talked to her. He never talked about himself and, if anyone asked him a personal question, he deflected it with the skill of someone who had done so many times.

Catherine studied him carefully and decided she liked him and that he was a decent man. He seemed kind, gentle and strong. He appeared not to have a care in the world but nor was he frivolous. He was affable with her customers and could hold his own in a discussion of politics, warfare, art, literature and music.

In contrast to many men who dedicate a significant proportion of their lives to sitting on bar stools he did not pontificate, he never became drunk or morose or in the least aggressive and he was a good listener. He took an interest in everyone and everything. He listened carefully to their stories and asked them intelligent questions. He was unfailingly polite, well-mannered and pleasant. He was clearly well read. He invariably carried with him an anthology of poetry with a scuffed leather cover and seemed to know much of it by heart. His memory was extraordinarily good until he was asked to remember something about himself, when he would suffer an attack of amnesia. Always the life and soul of the party, he was an attraction, measurably good for business. Customers came earlier and stayed to hear him talk. And the people who clustered round him paid nothing extra for the privilege. Jack always insisted on paying for his round of drinks. He also declined the many invitations he received to join customers who were staying for lunch or dinner.

After three weeks of almost continuous presence in the bar, Jack did not appear one lunchtime, nor did he come in that evening. Catherine felt unreasonably hurt that he had disappeared without a word of explanation (although she had to admit that he was beholden to no one). Then she felt anxious in case he had been taken ill. Then she started to feel something different altogether and it frightened her that he might never return.

She was mightily relieved when he appeared on the third day.

He said that he had been to an interview for a job and that he thought he would like it if it were offered to him. The opening was to run a landscape gardening business in Berkshire and she felt her heart sink at the prospect of his parting for good, but jobs in the post war years were hard to find. The country had been on a war footing for six years now. A huge number of ex-servicemen were now looking for work in a virtually bankrupt economy.

So Catherine congratulated Jack and said that if that was the job he really wanted she hoped he would get it.

Jack thanked her and said he should know the result in a few days. Then casually he said, out of the blue, 'I have been meaning to ask you; if I take the job, would you come with me?' Just like that.

Catherine says she does not know how or why she answered the way she did, but without hesitation she said, 'Yes, yes, I would like that. Yes.'

'By then I was in love with him, you see,' she says and the echo of the sound of her laughter bounces off a wall of sadness.

Catherine does not remember – or does not care to say much – about the last few weeks or days at the hotel but suddenly, there she was, transported to Windlesham according to the Electoral register of 1948, where she tried to find out more about the man she had just agreed to spend her life with.

Although she and Jack spent almost twenty years together, Jack remained an enigma.

She says he never told her where he came from and, when I say I find that hard to believe, she insists it is true, but he did tell her this much. He was twenty-one years older than her and he had been in the army all his adult life – longer in fact, for he had entered it as a sixteen year old, masquerading as eighteen. He told her that he had been in a long, deeply unhappy marriage; he said they had separated many years ago, which was fairly true, but she would never give him a divorce, which was probably the case. He also told her that they had no children (which was economical with the truth).

Catherine assumed from his family name, slight accent and marital inflexibility that he was from an Irish Catholic background. While his roots may have lain in Ireland, the records show that he was born and raised in England, but for some reason he would never confirm this. Similarly, he would never talk about what he had done in the War just ended, but said that his military service had finished with him spending almost a year in hospital, which suggested that he was not 'just the office boy'.

He never told her about being a decorated officer in the First World War when he was barely out of his teens; she discovered this by accident when tidying the bedroom. The medals were not hidden, just thrown casually into a chest of drawers with the rest of his meagre possessions. I have copies of the citations; here was Jack, my natural father, not as Catherine ever saw him nor the patrons of the hotel, but as a young soldier. Although his regiment escaped the carnage of Ypres there was fierce fighting up and down the line.

MILITARY CROSS

T/2Lt. Fred Simmons Tooley R. Ir. Rif

For conspicuous gallantry and devotion to duty when in command of a raiding party. He went forward in daylight and cut through five rows of the enemy's wires, and entered one of their posts, where he encountered a party of the enemy of twice his strength. His party put all the enemy out of action and brought back a prisoner. The success of this enterprise was entirely due to his forethought, extreme gallantry and rapid handling of the situation.

Place and date of deed S.W. of Havrincourt 9th October 1917.

And again;

BAR TO THE MILITARY CROSS

T/ Lt. (A./Capt.) Fred Simmons Tooley R. Ir. Rif

For conspicuous gallantry and devotion to duty. When the enemy had seized a village, this officer organised and led a counter-attack. After driving the enemy out, although he had only ten men left, he held the place against two attacks, withdrawing only when driven out by large forces of the enemy.

Place and date of deed Vert Galant 23 March 1918

There are a number of interesting points about these citations, apart from the fact that Jack was obviously courageous.

The first is that, having lied about his age to get into the army, as he told Catherine he had, he was a decorated officer by the time he was twenty-two. This seems unlikely until you walk around a cemetery such as Tyne Cot in Ypres and look at the age of many of the men buried there. Some of them were even younger. It also suggests very rapid promotion; second lieutenant to acting captain in the space of six months perhaps reflected both his leadership qualities and the appalling casualty rates.

I feel gratified by the use of the word gallantry. An old fashioned word, it suggests a combination of courage and honour and not just the actions of a young man who had lost his mind and simply run amok with a rifle or bayonet.

I can now start to see the way this story is headed. The eventual outcome comes into focus suddenly and ominously; it could all be summed up in one sentence, but having started I was determined not to distract Catherine from giving me a full account.

Given her indifference to the War, I suspect that the decorations meant far more to me than they did to her.

Later, she apologised for forgetting to tell me that he had also once mentioned casually being awarded some kind of 'gong' by the French while in hospital. This could have been the Croix de Guerre, but I have been unable to verify it.

Indeed, the decorations changed my perceptions of my father and of my past in a way she could not. I respect this. Catherine loved Jack unreservedly for what he was, then and there, and not because he was a decorated hero or because of what he had been. They calmed my fears that I was just a bastard child and the inconvenient result of promiscuous coupling in some dreary terraced house in Jericho, Oxford, abandoned because the child could not be aborted. That my natural father was a hero and not a drunk was comforting. It was a surprise to learn that he must have been almost sixty when I was born. This is not uncommon nowadays but it must have been rare in the 1950s.

Several times, Catherine said, she tried to raise the subject of his decorations but he rebuffed her, saying only that he had loved the army because of the outdoor life, the camaraderie and the travel but that eventually he hated the War, because of the friends he had lost – better men than him, he said. He had seen more than enough of war to know it was horrible, that you had to move on.

As to his role in World War Two, Catherine said that it must have been something on active service, even for a man in his late 40s. However, beyond some veiled comments about 'teaching the young 'uns' how to survive' he would not be drawn.

There is evidence that he re-enlisted in 1939 and further evidence that by 1944 he was adjutant and an instructor at the primary training centre in Guildford, on secondment from the Irish Rifles. This centre put new recruits through a gruelling and sometimes brutal twelve-week infantry course. The instructors were battle-hardened veterans who knew the reality of war. They were known by the recruits as seagulls, 'because they crapped all over you'. But how an instructor could sustain injuries from which it took a year to recover seems strange. Is it possible that he accompanied some of his charges who were sent to different regiments on the D-Day landings or the subsequent savage battle for Normandy? It would have been entirely in character.

When she asked him again about his wounds he just laughed it off, saying that he had fallen off a ladder. The deep scars on his back told a different story. Eventually, after her persistence made him angry (which was rare for him) she let the subject drop.

If Jack had been in the army today and had been badly wounded in, say, Afghanistan, the chances are that he would have received far better medical care in the first few crucial hours, that he would have gone to a specialist hospital and then to a rehabilitation centre. Eventually, when the time came to make big decisions, if he had been invalided out it would have been on the advice of a doctor and a psychiatrist, the latter probably having diagnosed PTSD (post-traumatic stress disorder). He would have been given a reasonable pension. In short, he would have received far better care. But this is now and that was then.

I have no reason at all to doubt that the doctors and nurses who looked after him when he was shipped back to England did the very best they could. But he was one amongst hundreds, if not thousands, and both their knowledge and their resources must have been stretched beyond limits.

If only they could move on, thought Catherine as she reflected on the momentous decision to live with Jack. But the fact was that she was now living with a badly damaged man.

Jack found it difficult to concentrate for long periods. He drank to excess and although he never became aggressive or even surly, she sensed sharp mood swings, including long periods when he fought depression. He remained devoted to her for the rest of his life, always kind, ever gentle, but Catherine came to realise he could see no future. A middle-aged puppy, he lived entirely for the moment, for the day, without a thought for tomorrow. He never planned, never saved, never worried about the future, perhaps because he knew that he had none. He was an engaging but irresponsible figure, who had left part of his mind, and part of his soul, in France. That he had once been an inspiration and a natural leader seemed beyond doubt; the medal citations bear witness to a courageous, impressive man. But do they also point to a reckless, self-destructive streak? He had admitted to her once that he was known as 'Mad Jack' to his men.

A characteristic that is an asset in wartime does not necessarily translate well into a time of peace. For men who have played an active role in not one but two world wars, the psychological consequences are hard to imagine. There must have been many thousands, no, hundreds of thousands of men, women and children who were pushed to the edge of sanity by

1945, by fear, grief and privation. However, that generation took a robust view of mental health, and Catherine's response was typical. 'You didn't think about that,' she said, 'you just got on with it as best you could.'

My adoptive father had a close friend who by coincidence was also called Jack, Jack Burnett. This Jack spent a year in Changi and two years on the Burma railway as a guest of the Japanese. My father said that the Jack who came home to Yorkshire at the end of the war bore little resemblance, either physically or in his behaviour, to the ambitious young textile executive who, by sheer misfortune, had chosen to visit Singapore at precisely the wrong moment and failed to get out. My father described a man who believed in nothing, valued nothing material that had no immediate practical use, and who lived for the day. He took up a place on a stool at the bar at Fixby Golf Club in Huddersfield and stayed there for the rest of his life.

As Catherine continued, her words triggered a memory; I have heard this story before I thought. If Rodin had been commissioned to create a sculpture to honour those who came home from the war damaged in body or mind, he would probably have called it 'le soldat au bar'.

Nevertheless, when Jack asked Catherine to go with him she agreed to do so without a moment's hesitation. Why?

Possibly because being much older he gave form to the father she had never known.

Possibly because in his naiveté, and palpable inability to cope with civilian life, he had a childlike quality, a vulnerability which brought out the protective, maternal instincts in her.

When I asked her this question, which was important to me, I found her answer vague, unsatisfactory. And so I asked her again, this time more directly, 'But Catherine why did you go and live openly with a man who was old enough to be your father, who was visibly ill, who drank far too much, had no job and no prospects of ever finding a decent one? Surely it wasn't out of sympathy? Surely you could have found a more eligible husband in Oxfordshire?' And it was true. Many men had stood at the bar and flirted with her. Some may have been oily spivs who had profited from the War while avoiding any risk to themselves. It is easy to understand why Catherine resisted their predations. But they cannot all have been unpleasant people.

In post-war Britain, which was virtually bankrupted by the conflict and would take a generation to recover, many girls in Catherine's situation would have married for love. But 'love' in a time of poverty, of drab houses, drab clothes and drab food, can acquire quite new semantics and come to mean financial security, warm houses, some variety in food (rationing ended only in 1952 although widely abused or ignored by those who could afford it). Few girls living in poverty would have resisted the allure of material reward as incentives to show affection to a man who could provide. But Catherine's only convincing explanation was, 'Because I already knew that I loved him,' followed by the little sardonic laugh that contained a world of misery.

When the job in Windlesham, Berkshire, did not work out, Catherine and Jack moved to Dorset in the summer of 1951 and set up home in the little cottage ('pretty run down' she sniffs, suddenly now on safer ground). They again set up home as husband and wife (which fooled nobody), and for a few brief months life appeared to be on an even keel.

However, the owners of the estate became concerned about Jack's work or, rather, lack of it. Word went around, as it does in rural communities, that 'the new chap they recruited from Berkshire wasn't up to it, was not pulling his weight.' And one day an important person from the big house came to see Jack in the evening and they went outside to talk.

Catherine overheard snatches of conversation: 'We know what you have been through... we shall all do our bit... but the work...'

Later, Jack came back inside; his customary jauntiness had vanished.

The next day he rose early and came home late, exhausted. He did the same thing the next day and next. But after ten days he was spent; he confessed to Catherine that he could not cope; this was clearly a job for a younger, fitter man. He went to bed and slept for two days. Then he said to Catherine he was very sorry but they had to leave.

The next part of her narrative was very short on detail, either on the day of our first meeting or in our later correspondence. It comes across as impressionistic and slightly surreal. Whenever I think of this memory it takes the form of a film, perhaps by David Lean. It opens with a vast panorama of a bleak, inimical countryside. The topography is central to the story.

This is a picture of a harsh, unforgiving landscape. This is nature, red in tooth and claw. It is Thomas Hardy but not the naïve young author of *Under the Greenwood Tree* or *The Woodlanders*. Those silly novels are populated by ruddy faced yokels who define the complex relationship between man and nature by dancing round a maypole, a look of idiotic contentment on their faces.

This, by contrast, is late Hardy, angry, brooding, disillusioned and deeply pessimistic. This is no bucolic idyll. It is Aeschylus set in the poverty of post-war 20th century rural

England. It is Egdon Heath and in a very real sense it is Lear's Heath, in which the wind and the rain lash those who walk on it, exposing the extent of human frailty.

Then the camera zooms in, sweeping the terrain, passing over the tops of trees and hedges and walls, until finally it picks out two tiny figures trudging slowly across the heath, their faces set hard against the elements. Hand in hand, and both badly wounded, they are walking towards the abyss.

Catherine and Jack ended up, God knows where, in a rented room in a remote village on the border of Dorset and Wiltshire. For a time, Catherine entered domestic service to support them.

Things were looking desperate because Jack's health was deteriorating and his hopes of finding work, any work at all, were receding.

Catherine became increasingly anxious and fearful of how they were going to cope. Things were bad enough before. But then came another challenge. Something else had happened that added to her feeling of hopelessness. In the autumn of 1953 Catherine discovered that she was pregnant.

Chapter 3 - My Childhood

My earliest memories are almost entirely happy. The handful of people still alive half a century later who remembered me during the first few years of my life recall a quiet, contented little boy who smiled often, seldom cried, slept soundly and showed not the slightest sign of having suffered a major trauma already in his brief life.

As time went by, my parents began to see other aspects of their son's character, including being accident-prone and a tendency, despite his habitual reserve, to attract attention.

One episode illustrated a certain defiance in my approach to life. Each year, my parents hosted a garden party for the members of the church they attended and other local luminaries. We had the biggest house with the biggest garden and while my father, a humble, rather shy man, had no interest in being seen as the local squire, he did have a sense of noblesse oblige. The garden party was held each year for many years in June and the sun always smiled on it. The guests sat around about a dozen trestle tables; these arrived mysteriously one or two days before, on the back of the lorry, and were taken away the next day. The parties were well attended. There was a speech by someone of stature, including on one occasion, the Bishop of Wakefield, and there were raffle prizes and games for the children. Although only tea was served, the garden parties always became boisterous towards the end at about six. At this point my parents would collapse into armchairs in the sitting room and say, 'Well, I think everyone enjoyed it, but it's a lot of hard work and I'm not sure we shall do another.' But, of course they did, for the next twenty years.

My parents put a huge effort into making a success of these events. And one year they became so involved that they took their eye off their son, aged about three and a half, who toddled out of the house and headed towards the garden party on the lawn. Along the side of the lawn was a steep bank which ran to another grass path and then into an orchard. Although we had an elderly gardener and although my father did his best, the garden always threatened to outgrow their efforts. And so it came to pass that, by the time of this particular garden party, the lawn looked impeccable but the path along the top of the bank was overgrown and the bank was a wilderness of brambles and nettles. Everyone was having a wonderful time and no one noticed a young Broadbent setting off down the path to the lawn. Instead of turning right, where he would have been perfectly safe wandering amongst the guests and enjoying the clucking attention of local matrons, for some reason he headed along the top of the bank. What no one had warned me was that half way along the top of the bank the pathway had collapsed but it was so covered in long grass no one had noticed. I was wearing shorts and my favourite sleeveless Tshirt and I waddled along as fast as I could go until, to my surprise, I stepped on a path that was no longer there and went head first straight down the forty foot bank, rolling over and over through brambles and thistles. I arrived at the bottom, more surprised than hurt but covered in scratches and bleeding profusely. As I lay there I became aware of shrieks of dismay and shouts of panic from the assembled guests. I was carried from the field of battle by a burly stranger and taken upstairs to my room. A doctor was called for and my multiple cuts and scratches were bathed in Dettol mixed with water and held in an enamel bowl. How vividly I remember the smell of Dettol and the white bowl with a blue rim. They are the culminating symbols of my early youth and used many times for similar purposes. On this occasion I saw a group of grown-ups round my bed looking concerned and kind. From somewhere, I have no idea where, my response to a crisis came quite naturally. 'Big boys don't cry,' I said which was clearly a smart thing to say because it sent the assembled adults into paroxysms of admiration. I lay there feeling sore but pleased with myself.

Many years later I would proudly declare my first words the equal of those attributed to Ernest Hemingway; 'fraid of nuthin'. Unfortunately for me, that was where the comparison ended.

However, my first years as a trainee Broadbent were very happy. I had a wonderful home, a huge garden to play in and loving parents. I was healthy. I could run all day, sleep soundly at night and suffered no bad dreams. Spring was good, summer better. And best of all was when it snowed heavily as it still did in those days. You would see the snowflakes start to fall in the late afternoon and knew that if the weather held, you would wake up and the first thing you would do would be to open the curtains and see the transformation of the garden from its dreary winter brown to a scene from the icing on Christmas cake. We (my sister and I) could not wait to get out to play, to dig out the back yard and all the way up the long drive to make a way for the postman and the milkman. The latter arrived on his float pulled by a magnificent Shire horse which, very sensibly, he left standing patiently up on the road while he gingerly walked down the drive himself.

In the evenings we would sit in the big drawing room listening to a performance of a Gilbert and Sullivan work on the wireless or to an LP by Flanders and Swann. And, to complete a perfect memory, there were always the two dogs lying by a real fire and gazing into the flames until they fell asleep. There were very few blemishes on my earliest years. As if pointing the way forward, we even had a silver tray with stags running round it that acquired an extra significance when I discovered T S Eliot. In short, I was happy.

Not so my sister Jane. Adopted four years earlier from different parents, she showed signs of not being at ease with herself very early on.

When she was thirteen she was sent away to a convent school in Whitby called St Hilda's. Her feelings about that institution make my attitude to my secondary school enthusiastic by comparison. With hindsight my parents admitted it was a mistake. Jane and the nuns were like oil and water. And despite being quite bright – highly articulate and with a flair for languages (and a brilliant mimic) – she failed to make any impression academically. She left school as soon as she could.

In those days, when we knew a great deal less than now about genetics, many people still believed that a new baby was a 'tabula rasa' on whom the parents could make the impression they wanted and set values and aspirations. Many parents have difficult children of their own, but often the delinquent behaviour patterns resolve themselves over time and a 'normal' relationship reasserts itself. I have not seen any authoritative research on the subject, but anecdotal evidence indicates a markedly higher proportion of adopted children displaying aberrant behaviour and that the older the child is when adopted, the higher the risk of it going seriously 'off piste'.

By the time my sister was in her early teens, a difficulty presented itself. She started to go out with men. This would be quite normal behaviour, except that all the men were much older than her and, in some cases, old enough to be her father. Inevitably these relationships ended badly. Having remained at home and qualified as a medical secretary, she headed off to London and then to Oxford, never staying in any job for more than two years but excelling in all of them.

Eventually she was working in a restaurant in Hertfordshire, by remarkable coincidence at a hotel and restaurant in Eaton Bray, Jack's birthplace. The owner's wife had recently died of cancer. He showed an interest in her. Although he was more than thirty years older than her, they married and went to live in Mallorca. There they had two children, Sarah and James, but after thirteen years, the marriage turned sour and she returned to the UK. It does not require the intellect of a Freud or a Jung to see that this odyssey of places and relationships was a fruitless search to find or replace her father.

Jane has been a kind, generous and loyal sister to me for most of our lives, although we seldom meet because we live at opposite ends of the country. We remain fairly close though we disagree about the importance of separation and adoption in our lives. She accepts that they were important in her early years but argues that they are a long forgotten part of the past. She now lives in Cumbria and is in a stable marriage to a talented artist of similar age.

It was pure chance that brought my sister and me together under the same roof and it is no surprise that our lives have followed very different paths. But we had a shared family life. It was a further spinning of Fortune's Wheel (which seems to have had several punctures during my brief life), that came to a shuddering halt, landing on the town of Huddersfield, West Yorkshire, and on the modest house (soon to be upgraded) of Theo and Margery Broadbent – my parents.

There have been Broadbents in that part of Britain since time immemorial. As a tribe, the Broadbents throughout their history have been stolid, decent, honest, conventional family-oriented people. They have been deeply devout Christians who attended church, often joined it, and practised what they preached. Although not intellectuals, indeed with a tendency to be anti-intellectual, they were on the whole well educated. Most of the men (and eventually most of the women) went to university, the majority to Oxford. And, in a graphic illustration of the risks of making premature judgements about people, I once branded one of my father's cousins the most tedious man I ever met. I would have had him down as a middle-ranking accountant in Surbiton. In fact, he was a senior officer in MI5 and had a first-rate intellect.

Nevertheless, it is a fact that few Broadbents ever made it out of the impoverished middle classes or even tried to – the selfish gene that determines financial and commercial acumen was sadly lacking. Instead they became soldiers, doctors in working class areas and clergymen in poor parishes. Since I felt no such calling, I often thought it perverse that articulate, well-educated people would chose such drab lives when with their background they could at least have become civil service mandarins or held senior marketing jobs in companies like Shell, BP or ICI. But they were blessed (or was it cursed?) with a strong sense of duty.

The Broadbents were patriots to a man (or to woman for that matter) and, it must be admitted, slightly xenophobic (with 'foreign' defined as anywhere outside West Yorkshire). They were conservative by nature, nurture, inclination and instinct. They liked cricket, and rugby union, thought rugby league a sad aberration and disliked football intensely. They enjoyed walking in the Lake District and trying to keep warm on the beaches of Cornwall and they spent their evenings playing the piano, listening to music or reading. Their tastes were catholic but tended towards lowbrow; they were more likely to include C. S. Forester, Henry Rider Haggard and John Buchan in their collections than James Joyce or Flaubert. They were disgusted by D. H. Lawrence's *Lady Chatterley's Lover* and by John Cleland's *Fanny Hill* and therefore did not read them. And even after a mini diaspora following radical changes in the textile industry, no Broadbent, at least as far as I know, ever voted anything other than Conservative. No Broadbent was ever caught hiding a volume of Marx under his copy of the *Daily Telegraph*. Even after they had emigrated to Bromley or Croydon, they retained a remarkable homogeneity of appearance and thought. And so, when the clan gathered for a wedding or funeral, one could wander round amongst the dog collars and have the same conversation half a dozen times with people who all looked bafflingly familiar.

Much later, as an adolescent with a strong naughty streak, I tried to identify at least one black sheep in the family with whom I could identify and went up and down the family tree in search of a libertine, a roué, a louche who had been expelled from school and fled to Paris, living in a garret in the Latin Quarter and writing a novel like *The Outsider*. I drew a blank. Not one, they were all good people. All of them.

So, I tried again to find a link between our family's history and an anti-heroic past. One of several keen genealogists in the family, perhaps the least reliable, claimed to have found circumstantial evidence that the bloodline was strengthened in the 8th century by an influx of Norsemen from Scandinavia. This was more like it. I found the idea exciting. And although there is not a single reference to Erik 'Bloodaxe' Broadbent in any recorded history, I held on to the possibility of a Viking infusion because it seems to add a touch of romance and devilry to an otherwise dull story.

In fact, the Vikings might not have provided the solution to my problem. Revisionist historians have argued the mythology is exactly that, a myth. They argue that the horned helmets, the axes, the rape and pillage are a fiction, a smear campaign by early Christians who briefed against the Vikings because the competition from Norse gods such as Thor and Odin was strong. We are now led to believe that having moored their longships neatly on the east coast (in what became Bridlington and Filey), they made their way to York, where they spent some time admiring the architecture, which was of Roman origin and far superior to anything you could see in Stavanger even today. They proceeded to trade peacefully with the locals and then, rather than outstay their welcome, they headed west, where they were assimilated into the communities they found there. In time they became estate agents, accountants and quantity surveyors in genteel towns such as Harrogate.

With or without a rich family tree, there was one gene that ran through generation after generation of Broadbents. Without any exception that I have ever discovered they were always kind people; kind to their children, their siblings, their colleagues, their employees and each other. This pervasive kindness shines like a beacon in an unkind world. In due course (but not, to my shame, for many years), that quality was to make me proud to carry the family name.

The major figure in the modern history of the family was the man known, to his and all future generations, as Great Uncle Ben. Exceptionally, he was a businessman and an able one at that. In some respects, he must have been the archetypal northern mill owner with a Yorkshireman's eye on costs and a canny eye for the main chance. However, by the standards of the time he treated his workforce well. I doubt he looked to Dickens or to Heinrich Heine to inform him of the condition of the poor in industrialised northern England; the evidence lay all around him but, without proposing radical solutions, he did what he could to improve their lot. His correspondence suggests a deep admiration for the great Quaker families; the Terrys in York, the Cadburys and the Barclays and their schemes to care for their workers through better housing, better health care and better sanitation. Ben's sense of social responsibility did not match theirs, his thinking was less radical, but neither was it mere tokenism, it was more a deep sense of 'noblesse oblige'. He was well known in Huddersfield for his philanthropy and numerous schools, hospitals and leisure facilities in the town still carry plaques that acknowledge the generosity of Benjamin Broadbent.

I doubt that Great Uncle Ben would have approved of the diktat, surely apocryphal, but often ascribed to the northern mill owner, that pregnant women giving birth should do so beside their loom in the weaving sheds and be back at work within hours or risk losing their jobs. I think it unlikely. His portraits depict a strong, stern man but not a cruel one... the eyes are kind.

He was knighted for his good works and the name Broadbent was respected even in the sad, post-industrialisation period of Huddersfield.

Uncle Ben was laid to rest in an enormous, gothic tomb. Well into the 1960s, if one happened to be passing, it was common to see flowers on the grave left by strangers.

The more cynical observer might say that Ben Broadbent could afford to be generous. He presided over his mills when Huddersfield and towns like it were in a golden age. Soft water and know how, and a strong work ethic, brought great wealth to that part of England. Its heyday was the late 1800s and the first three decades of the 20th century as England, more particularly Yorkshire, was the world's leading producer of wool textiles. His flagship, Parkwood Mill, and a few others like it, produced of some of the world's finest worsted, much of it destined for Savile Row. In addition to this stream of income, he won huge contracts to produce uniform material for the armed forces.

Huddersfield grew rich and, as the mansions in the more fashionable areas such as Egerton bear witness; the mill owners knew how to celebrate their success.

Visiting the two places now, it seems extraordinary that Huddersfield and Bradford vied with each other in the 1920s as to which had the greatest number of Rolls Royces in Britain. The winner even today is disputed, but the Broadbents always believed their home town edged it for most of the decade. After all, Great Uncle Ben had two.

The gilded age of the West Riding was short lived. There was already a marked sea change by the time I was born and the rapid decline accelerated in the 1960s and 1970s. For a while the influx of immigrants from India, Pakistan and Bangladesh, many of whom went to work in the mills, helped to keep the industry afloat by keeping labour costs down. But they only served to plaster over the cracks and to delay the inevitable. The same countries that had provided the migrants had also improved their technology and could produce cloth on a massive scale.

Something else important happened too – denim. Fashions changed rapidly in the 1960s. The young people in the western world, and soon it seemed on the entire planet, no longer wanted to wear suits, certainly not in their increasing leisure time. High street names like Burton and Hepworth disappeared, to be replaced by new names such as Levi's and Wrangler. In less than a generation, towns like Huddersfield went from industrial to post-industrial as traditional industries were hollowed out.

In many cases, managers with a parochial view of the world did not see change coming until it was too late; it is unlikely that they could have done much even if they tried, which most of them didn't. Across the Pennines the cotton industry of Lancashire was hit hard too and towns like Oldham, Blackburn and Bury have never recovered.

The decline of the textile industry in Yorkshire brought with it the decline of the great textile dynasties, including the Broadbents (who to be fair were never in the top rank in terms of size). Smarter than most and shrewd until the end, Ben still saw a future for high end textiles and refocused his business accordingly.

If, in the late 1980s, you were to drive up the valley where the biggest mills used to be, you would see every mile or so a huge pile of rubble where a mill and its tall chimney had once stood. It was an industrial archaeologist's version of an elephant's graveyard, a reminder of how it used to be. Only when you neared the top of the valley, just below the reservoir that used to supply all the thirsty mills in the valley, would you see the last survivor and that was Parkwood.

I like to think of it is a tribute to my father, who managed it for thirty years. Prompted by the problems posed by the effluents from the dyeing process he turned his practical mind to developing a series of mechanical screens and established a highly successful environmental engineering division called the Longwood Engineering Company. Its products, for which he obtained several patents, were in demand all over the world and, for several years, its profits shored up the ailing mill, which partly explains why it lasted as long as it did.

Eventually, a large company based in the south east of England offered to buy the business and the patents. Selling it would have made my father a very wealthy man, but he declined the offer because he didn't want to leave Yorkshire and because he felt that it would be disloyal to his workers.

A few years ago, my dear friend Glen drove us up there to have what I thought was a last look at the great mill building. I had walked through it many times as a child, completely unable to hear a word of what anyone said because of the deafening noise of the machinery. It was now absolutely silent but prompted memories of the past.

I remembered with pleasure how my father had shown round visiting dignitaries. The tour began in the yard where the huge bales of wool arrived, as sheared from the sheep, and went through the various processes of washing, dyeing, more washing, carding, teasing, spinning, weaving and finishing until, at the other end, you could touch some of the finest material in the world before it was sent down to Savile Row. I think my father would have been pleased that the building still stood, but mortified that it had been converted into 'executive flats'.

The decline of the textile industry marked the end of the most prosperous period in the clan's history, yet it had little effect on the rest of the Broadbents who, although now unlikely to enjoy large inheritances, blithely went on ploughing the same old furrow.

My paternal grandfather, Henry Stuart, was a clergyman who for many years before and after the Great War served in depressed areas of Liverpool. However, although he never applied for missionary work, he also spent three years in the unlikely parish of Saskatoon, Canada. No one seems to know or will admit why he had been sent there.

My own, uncorroborated, theory is that he had spent a large part of the Great War ministering to the thousands of wounded men brought to the huge casualty clearing station at Étaples. Some were shipped back to recover in England, many were buried in France (the military cemetery there contains some 11,500 graves). My guess is that my grandfather, who was a quiet, very sensitive man, had suffered some kind of breakdown as a result of what he saw there. The Broadbents, being a strong military family with the stiffest of upper lips, would have been embarrassed by this display of weakness, in a

78

man who had not even served in the trenches. They may have arranged for him to go abroad to convalesce and not to come back until he was ready. So my father was born a Canadian 'in the saddle,' as he liked to jest, but that branch of the family was, if not shunned exactly, ignored.

The clan had found a far more suitable hero in Great Uncle Ken who won three DSOs in the Great War and was twice recommended for the VC. It is said that only his position as both a doctor and a chaplain made him a non-combatant and (just) ineligible. The Victoria Cross and Bar has only ever been awarded to three men, two of them in the 1914-18 War and both of them doctors. The more I read about Noel Chavasse the more I revered Great Uncle Ken. The only significant difference between them that I could see, was that Chavasse died winning his second decoration, while Great Uncle Ken miraculously survived and moved on to the rest of his serenely lived life, dying in his sleep at home at the age of 94.

I met him only twice, at his home in Scotland. I was so in awe of him that the first time I met him I became completely tongue-tied. He was the kindest, gentlest of men.

The next time we visited him, he took me down to the river that ran past the end of his garden and in pouring rain, patiently explained to me the essential elements of fly-fishing. He had a radiant serenity that I have seen in no other human being. He was the best a man can be.

Poor Grandpa by contrast was a tortured soul. He lived with us for many years until I went away to school and my long-suffering mother could no longer cope with him. My parents used to find him irascible and rather regretted giving him a home. I was very fond of him, but he used to retreat into his room and not come out for days on end. I now think he was clinically depressed. The only person who shared this suspicion about my grandfather's state of mind was my favourite aunt, the wife (now widow) of my father's youngest brother. Her father was Field Marshal Montgomery's chaplain during the Second World War and later Chaplain General of the army, before retiring some years after the war to take up the comparative sinecure of Dean of Ripon Cathedral. She was a nurse and more than anyone may have known the real story. My father may have known something, but when I tried to raise the subject he dismissed it as 'arrant tripe' and, if pressed, he became evasive and irritable.

In any event my grandfather left Canada and returned to Liverpool when my father was about three years old. All five sons were raised there, until my father was seventeen. Then, perhaps as a reward for all the hard years ministering in the working-class areas of Liverpool (the vicarage backed onto Scotland Road which averaged a murder a night), Grandpa was appointed vicar to an easier, more prosperous parish in Tanfield, North Yorkshire.

Broadbents are nothing if not conventional, and my father's four brothers all went into 'approved' professions. One became a doctor, two became clergymen, one joined the army. Three had been to Oxford, one to Cambridge. The odd man out, which was unusual for him, was my father, who by common consent was the brightest of all of them. He spurned a place at Oxford, and instead went to Leeds University, where he read Mining Engineering. At the time he graduated there was talk of him joining the family business, which at the time was being managed by his Uncle Eddie. However, the latter was still some way off retirement so it was decided that my father would shadow his uncle for a year or so, then go and see something of the world, develop his character and add to his management skills through a short-term commission in the army.

In those days, young people of a certain class used to go regularly to dance halls and enjoy evenings of low alcohol and considerable propriety under the watchful eye of responsible adults of some seniority. My father was an athletic man who had been a mountaineer and an oarsman who rowed for his university. He loved dancing and was a regular attendee while on attachment in Huddersfield. He made good friends with like-minded men with shared interests. One of them was Kenneth Turner who became his lifelong best friend. The other was a young man who harboured an ambition the others thought absurd – to become an actor. His name was James Mason.

As things turned out Kenneth became a Huddersfield solicitor, my father became the managing director of a declining textile mill and James Mason went to Hollywood and appeared or starred in a score of major movies, including *The Blue Max* with Ursula Andress.

After I heard this I ceased to believe in any concept of a just God. For many years I refused my parents' endless requests to take dancing lessons; I thought it unlikely that I would meet Ursula Andress in the YMCA Huddersfield.

As it turned out, things didn't quite go to plan. My father's short-term commission coincided with the outbreak of the Second World War. He stayed on in the army for much longer than originally intended, while his Uncle Eddie continued at the mill longer than he had planned.

My poor mother, a clergyman's daughter from Oldham, whom my father had met at Tanfield through mutual friends and married in haste and against both sets of parents' wishes ('You are both far too young'), was left to cope on her own with her ageing parents for far too long. She was the kindest, most generous, warm-hearted person I ever knew. She was also a devout Christian and there is no doubt that her faith sustained her in the difficult years ahead. After the war she would devote much of the time working for the SSAFA (Soldiers, Seamen, Airmen, and Families Association), the armed forces charity.

If you had asked either of my adoptive parents what the greatest achievement of their life had been, they would both have said it was their fifty-five-year marriage. I grew up thinking all marriages were like that; warm, loving, supportive and tolerant. It was some time before I was disabused of the notion.

My father enjoyed soldiering, probably more than he had any right to. He was brave and he was clever and had a certain quiet authority that marked him out as a natural leader. He had an instinctive feel for machinery and many years later his map reading skills would leave me gasping with admiration during our walks in the Lake District together. He loved Ordnance Survey one inch to the mile maps, which he would pore over for hours, absorbing every detail.

He always said that being in the army simplified life, especially when you were at war. You only had two things to think about; killing the enemy while staying alive yourself. He said you always knew what you had to do and why you had to do it. He confessed to leaving the army with mixed feelings, especially as he had been enjoying himself after Germany's surrender, running a large part of Schleswig Holstein under the army of occupation.

Looking back over his life he probably made the wrong decision; he loved the army and the army loved him. He always found civilian life dull, complex, baffling. His favourite brother, Colin, did join the army and made a good career moving steadily through the ranks and finishing up a colonel before disappearing into the secret world for a few more years prior to his retirement. To my great envy, Uncle Colin took his family on overseas postings in Germany, Australia and Hong Kong. My father had little interest in business and even less in making money, but it is highly unlikely that, with his background, intellect and already a major in his mid-twenties, he would not have ended up as a full colonel, if not a brigadier. Even peacetime armies have some opportunities for advancement. The one limitation might have been my mother, who would not have enjoyed the vacuous braying of the officers' mess and judged 'overseas' as suitable for holidays and not much else.

Despite the charms of army life, my father decided to honour the commitment he had made to the family when the war began that, when it was over, he would come home to Huddersfield and take over the running of the mill, allowing Uncle Eddie finally to retire.

My mother was delighted. She would have supported my father whatever he did, but by nature was not ideally suited to being an army wife. She was profoundly grateful to have him home alive and in one piece and to stay in Yorkshire.

And there were compensations. Shortly after taking over as managing director at the mill, his great Aunt Sarah gifted my father a fine house with several acres of grounds, including land that bordered a big reservoir that fed the mills. The reservoir had been formed, in a formidable piece of early Victorian engineering, by building a dam across the upper reaches of a narrow valley. If you stood on the dam and looked east you could see all the way down the valley, past Parkwood Mill and the piles of rubble, to the town itself about four miles way. Looking west, there was a wood through which ran a stream which fed the reservoir, and beyond that there was open countryside, the moors of Ian Brady and Myra Hindley notoriety and the badlands of Lancashire.

My father, a placid, naturally contented man, was not given to regrets. Although he talked often about the Second World War he always maintained that he did not miss the army. He said that the annual regimental reunions, that he never failed to attend, were all he needed to sustain him. And so, he and my mother moved into the big house that was called Oakscar and lived there happily ever after. Almost.

It is a truth universally recognised that a man in possession of a declining mill, a big house, a small salary and a loving wife must be in need of children. Although my parents were married shortly before the start of the War and my father had enjoyed periods of home leave, they had been unable to start a family. For whatever reason (I never knew why), they remained unable to do so although they tried for several years after. They knew that time was against them. My mother had just turned forty, which in those days was considered dangerously old to have a child. Now, anxious to secure the one thing still wanted, they decided to take action. They contacted a close friend of my mother, Betty Armitage.

Betty and my mother had started nursing training together, but to her great regret my mother had had to abandon her career in order to care for her elderly parents. Betty, on the other hand, had gone from strength to strength. She was a formidable woman who had made a name for herself caring for the injured in the East End of London during the Blitz. She was on her way to becoming matron of the South London Hospital, and eventually one of the most senior nurses in the NHS. However, at that time she was working at the Radcliffe Infirmary in Oxford, where she was the sister in charge of the maternity ward. She was present at my sister Jane's birth and at mine.

She was a good friend (gossip had it that she was a very good friend) of the hospital's senior obstetrician, Sir John Stallworthy.

I am not sure how it came about, and my parents were the last people ever to break the law, but the normal application and approval process for adoption, which was and is usually protracted and intrusive, was somehow shortened (probably shrinking under Betty's withering gaze). My parents made two quick trips to Oxford (on each occasion spending one night at the Mitre) and our family was complete.

My sister and I were too young to remember being introduced to our parents, and neither of us can remember being told we had been adopted. I can remember sharing this important piece of information with a friend at my primary school and feeling crestfallen when he did not seem remotely impressed. I don't think either of us understood what it meant.

For the next twenty years or so I wasn't particularly impressed myself. In fact, I thought little about it and, when I did, I told myself what my parents and Betty Armitage had told me; that it was of no consequence. I am quite sure that they believed it.

Once or twice in my early teens I asked my mother about it and she was entirely relaxed and not in the least defensive. I remember her telling me, quite correctly, that my natural father was a war hero, that he and my mother were in a long term stable relationship, but that he was already married to someone who would not give him a divorce. All of which was probably accurate. She also told me that Jane's parents were high born and that her arrival in the world was a suppressed society scandal of some significance. That was probably true too.

However, I do not think my parents, or anyone else for that matter, thought at that time that the circumstances of our adoption were of the slightest importance. They did make some allowance for nature but voted overwhelmingly in favour of nurture. All they knew was that they now had a complete family and, from the moment they adopted us, they loved us unconditionally and they were blissfully happy to have two physically healthy children, tabulae rasae, to bring up as decent, law abiding, conservative, traditional Broadbents, upon whom they could leave the print marks of good Christians.

For our part, I do not think that either my sister or I ever had the slightest doubts about who were Mum and Dad. It was just that there was always an itch that needed scratching and it never quite went away.

But for the next twenty plus years I gave the matter little thought and, when I did, I dismissed it as of no consequence. After all, I was busy getting on with life.

Chapter 4 - Boyhood

'Issues from the hand of God, the simple soul
To a flat world of changing lights and noise.'
T S Eliot, *Animula*

The world I grew up in was kind, strict and stable. It was loving but undemonstratively so. It was sane, well mannered and principled and recognised a clear line of demarcation between right and wrong. There was a well-scrubbed decency about the name Broadbent and it was thoroughly deserved.

Oakscar was a happy home and a marvellous house to grow up in. The grounds consisted of an area at the front of the house that was fully under control and cultivated and bedded with narcissi and azaleas. This area would have been quite big enough on its own but Aunt Sarah's gift was munificent. In addition, there was a big kitchen garden, an orchard, a wood and a field, the last two bordering the reservoir. In total, we had about four acres. I spent much of my early life in those gardens and knew every square inch of them.

Sometimes I played by myself giving free rein to my imagination, sometimes with friends. My two main friends at this time were Victor and Van Southwart, the two sons of the local publican. I lost touch with them when I went away to school and, while I have no idea what became of Van, when I was about eighteen I picked up and followed Victor's burgeoning career as a professional rugby league player. I had felt his strength during many robust games in the woods and the field and it gave me a foretaste of what was to come.

The house itself was big, but it had only four bedrooms because the whole of the middle was hollowed out in a spectacular atrium in which a staircase ran up two sides to a landing beneath an enormous skylight. In keeping with the family ethos, the walls were decorated with weaponry from various wars in which the Broadbents had fought. There was a musket from the Khyber Pass, swords from Afghanistan, a First World War bayonet, samurai swords captured in the Second World War, a huge sabre with which one of my ancestors is alleged to have cut in half, with one blow, an Indian mutineer (even *I* thought this story unlikely, although for a while it rekindled my enthusiasm for warriors).

On the second part of the staircase, on the other side of a grandfather clock, were the latest additions; ceremonial officers' swords and daggers from the Wehrmacht, the Kriegsmarine, the Luftwaffe and the SS, all of which my father had looted from his parish in Schleswig Holstein. In showing off the collection, of which he was inordinately proud, he used to say that the Wehrmacht officers who had surrendered to him were correct and professional, but the SS were arrogant and had not accepted they were beaten. He said that he would have enjoyed strangling personally a senior member of the Hitler Youth, captured in the area. Since my father rarely spoke ill of anyone, this gentleman must have had some special qualities.

With all this hardware hanging from the walls it sounds as if Oakscar was made to look like a poor imitation of a Scottish castle, but it was not at all like that and I loved the place and so did the many visitors who came to stay.

At Christmas we always had a huge tree about twelve feet tall. My sister and I used to decorate it and you had to go up the staircase to reach the upper branches and put the star on top. And every year we hosted a carol service for about thirty singers, a number of them from the renowned Huddersfield Choral Society. Given the friendly acoustics and that the singing was first class the result was impressive. Afterwards the singers would stay for mince pies and mulled wine, before thanking us for our hospitality and trudging happily up the drive in the snow. After we left Oakscar Christmas was never the same again.

The Christmas presents I received generally had a military theme. There was a marvellous collection of lead soldiers which had been given to my father and which he gave to me. These were displayed in a glass cabinet and treated with reverence. They were not toys to be played with. For fun, I had a generous allocation of plastic soldiers which I used to place all the way up the first part of the staircase and then take up a position about 150 feet away, near the front door, and attack them with a collection of guns, tanks and rockets that I had received as presents at previous Christmases and birthdays. My father would look on approvingly and explain some of the finer points of gunnery, such as range finding, trajectory angles, firing rates, killing ratios. My parents had no sense of modern political correctness and, since guns were all I wanted, guns were what I got. I became quite proficient, although not half as good as my cousin Andy, who went on to take a prize at Bisley and to train to fly helicopter gunships.

At the age of about eight I discovered an interest in angling. This was hardly surprising, given the proximity of a large area of water stocked with pike, perch and roach, some of them of prize-winning proportions. As was the way with me, my interest rapidly turned into an obsession and I spent every spare moment I had for the next few years trying to catch the big one. There was believed to be an enormous pike in the reservoir called Uncle Sam, but although I did once see a huge pair of jaws emerge from the water and take a moorhen under, I am not certain I ever saw him, much less got a hook into him. (Fishing remained a lifelong interest and some of my most contented hours have been spent on Ladybower reservoir in

Derbyshire with my dear friend John Moore, in pursuit of elusive trout.)

The day came when my childhood idyll was rudely interrupted by the need to get an education and, at the age of four, I joined my sister at a primary school in Huddersfield called the Mount School.

My school days did not begin well and for someone supposed to possess a remarkable memory, my recollections of the Mount are surprisingly vague. I attribute this to the fact that I loathed the place and my conscious mind has done its best to suppress or eradicate all memory of it. The core problem was my weakness in Mathematics.

I showed distinct early promise in English and that was recognised, but even rudimentary Maths left me completely mystified. And the more I failed the tests, the more Mrs Wright, the desiccated old hag of a Maths teacher, vented her self-loathing by hurling abuse at me. She humiliated me repeatedly in front of the entire class and then persuaded Ms Theobald, the black clad, chain-smoking headmistress, and a functioning alcoholic, that it would be of benefit if she weighed in and humiliated me in front of the entire school. Ms Theobald obliged.

I have hated very few people in my life, and even fewer have actually wronged me, but to this day I believe that, if Fate should provide the opportunity I would enjoy garrotting both Mrs Wright and Ms Theobald. By sheer coincidence my mother met Annie Wright many years later, just before my wedding, and the following week she sent a present that, if I remember, was a glass bell. When we opened it and saw who it was from I walked out of the house and threw it straight in the bin.

My parents remonstrated with me, scolding me for such ingratitude. 'She is an old lady now,' my mother said, 'she is delighted you have done so well. You must move on; surely the time has come to bury the hatchet.'

'The only place I would bury the hatchet is in that bitch's head,' I replied. 'I wouldn't have been surprised if she had sent us a voodoo doll.'

It was only then my parents really grasped the extent of my loathing or that their son could be so un-Christian. It should have served as a warning.

I have the greatest sympathy for people with dyslexia who, before the condition was identified and given a name, were treated as I was treated, as miscreants or imbeciles. One might have expected someone, an experienced teacher perhaps, to have stopped asking their poor student questions they simply could not answer and asked themselves a few instead. Many years later, I was talking to, of all people, a charming Professor of Mathematics at Cambridge. I assumed that she would react to my confession of early innumeracy as others had done, with a look of amusement or contempt, particularly as I was working for an international bank at the time. But to my surprise, she looked at me sympathetically and asked some more searching questions. 'I suspect that what you were suffering from was infantile dyscalculia,' she said at last. 'It is a much less common, numerical equivalent of dyslexia but it is a real condition. Like dyslexia it is often counterbalanced by above average aptitude in other directions.'

I sensed the pure pleasure of vindication washing over me.

'And did you eventually grow out of it?' she asked.

'Yes,' I said, I had, and I explained that I worked for a bank, a career choice that at one time would have resulted in hysterical laughter amongst my friends. It was true; although no mathematical genius, I had grown quite accustomed to pages of figures that at one time might have appeared as a blur. I had no problem reading a balance sheet or managing a budget of several million pounds.

However, the road to redemption had been long and unnecessarily hard. It was left to a far-sighted house tutor at Sedbergh (not my next school, but the one after that) to first recognise that I might have a problem that was something other than pure or even deliberate stupidity. By then I was displaying considerable academic potential but I needed to pass Maths O level. Everyone does because it is rightly considered a basic skill in life. The tutor, whose job it was to oversee the general wellbeing of the boys in his house and to support the housemaster, was an amiable man called Tony Thomas. Much shrewder and more insightful than he was given credit for, he was the first person to sense that I had a problem – other than being a congenital idiot. He also had the wisdom to see that, surprisingly, the appropriate response might not be routine abuse and humiliation and that I might benefit from a little help. 'Michael,' he said, 'it puzzles me; you are clearly going to be outstanding in some subjects and while it is quite normal to have an intellectual bias, I hope you will forgive me if I say you are unusually lopsided and listing badly in your Maths, which is well below average.'

'I know sir,' I replied. 'It drives me to distraction. If I look at a page of numbers they just swim before my eyes and my mind goes completely blank. I think I must have had a difficult birth or something. And the harder I try the worse it gets, and then I become anxious and that triggers a vicious circle.'

'Well,' he said, smiling benevolently, 'let me coach you so that you can at least get an O level. Then you can concentrate on the things you are really good at and leave all the rest behind.'

And that is exactly what happened. Little by little, under his patient tutelage, the scales fell from my eyes. I passed my Maths O level with room to spare.

Years after I left school I heard that Tony Thomas had been appointed headmaster of a major public school for girls. I was delighted for him, although I sometimes wonder how it is that Annie Wright and Tony Thomas ended up in the same profession.

But I am getting ahead of myself. When I was eight years old, my parents sent me away to boarding school in Cumbria. This is not every parent's ideal of the best way to bring up their children or to bond with them. Many mothers and more than a few fathers feel that it is way too soon to sever the second, invisible umbilical cord which otherwise may remain in place until the child leaves the nest in their 20s and sometimes even later.

Indeed, to some parents the whole concept of boarding school is anathema, an unwanted relic of a lost Empire. 'Why bother to have children at all,' they say, 'if you are going to send them away and effectively lose the best years, when you could really enjoy them as well as building a lifelong bond? Besides, in many areas the local state schools have academic records that are equal to or better than their fee-paying neighbours? It is unnatural and downright cruel to abandon a child at that age when they can fall prey to bullying or worse.'

These people have a point; being sent to a boarding school at the age of eight does change the parent-child dynamic forever.

On the other side is a group (I hesitate to say class although social class is often a factor) which argues that separation before adulthood is in keeping with nature, that most animals leave their offspring to fend for themselves before they reach full maturity and understand the dangers of the surrounding environment. These people believe it healthy to unshackle the child, thereby allowing it the opportunity to take early lessons in self-reliance. They may debate the optimum age for releasing the child into the wild, some favouring eight, some at thirteen, but they agreed on the principle. In addition, there are many in this group who claim that there are real benefits in a boarding school. In the absence of any realistic alternative they need to convince themselves that, if you are a member of the armed forces, or a diplomat, or working for a company such as Schlumberger or Hongkong Bank, where you can expect to move house every two to three years, that continuity and quality of education may well be preferable to changing schools a dozen times. Critics of boarding schools (and they are many and they are vocal), would do well to remember the reality of some people's lives. If you are a geologist trying to find oil in the middle of a jungle in Borneo, you would have to wait a long time to hear the cheerful hooting of the school bus in the morning.

For all these reasons, England's public schools host a large number of children from expatriate families, as well as a growing number of foreign students; the sons and daughters of wealthy Chinese, Malaysians or Nigerians prepared to pay a premium to secure 'an English education'.

There is one other factor; cost. Many expatriates receive a large subsidy for the cost of putting their children through boarding school. It can vary between a third and two thirds of the total. Whatever the amount, it is a major factor in the decision to stay abroad for as long as possible and it brings private education within the range of people who, if they were employed in the UK, would have to make enormous sacrifices to send their children away to school. Those parents who are based in the UK tend to be successful professionals or the senior executives of large companies. These are the few people who can find the school fees on taxed income.

Unfortunately, my father fell into neither category, and since there was no hope of a revival in the textile industry he paid himself a pittance. We may have lived in a big house but my parents were always flat broke. Nevertheless, they were absolutely determined from the outset that both my sister and I should go away to school, even though they must have known that it would beggar them. If you had asked them why it was considered so important to make such a huge sacrifice, my father, intelligent man though he was, would have shrugged and given a typical Broadbentian answer. 'Never really thought about it,' he would have said. 'It's what we always did. As you know, I went to and enjoyed Sedbergh; so did my four brothers, so did your grandfather and his father before him. I put your name down for the school when you were three months old. It's a tradition. It's what Broadbents always do.' Like voting Conservative and taking holidays in Cornwall. And going to church on Sundays. And being kind.

Brilliant though he was as an engineer and designer of machines, my father saw life in simple terms. Had he ever been called upon to justify his decision – and he never was – he would have made a strong case. It was divided into three parts.

First, my parents were determined to give us the best start in life. That meant the best education at the best schools they could find. To my father that meant a high standard of teaching and good academic grades.

Secondly, it also meant something else. He wanted a school that turned out good people. And although he might, very reluctantly and in the face of powerful statistics, have conceded the state system could and often did achieve high academic standards, he yielded to no-one in his belief that private education was incomparably better at shaping character

100

than going to a day school. I believe that he had a clear image in his mind of what a good person should be and that his old school, Sedbergh, was the place most likely to produce them. I think the ideal to which he aspired was a cross between Great Uncle Ken and Lord Baden Powell. He did not claim that any Broadbent had achieved such a level of human perfection but that was the ideal and Sedbergh was the anvil on which such a superman might be forged. The discovery that his only son had aspirations of a different nature would have shocked and disappointed him.

Thirdly, he held the charming but naïve belief that an education at Sedbergh would establish one in society and open all sorts of doors. The only doors I ever discovered at Sedbergh led to Sandhurst or agricultural college. His belief in the institution was founded on an illusion that Sedbergh was in the same bracket as Eton and Winchester, which was patently not the case. But my father was a northerner with a northerner's perspective and while Sedbergh stood, and still stands, in the first rank of northern public schools, when it came to it, it did not feature in the minds of people who lived or worked in Westminster or in Kensington and Chelsea.

However, first things first. The preparatory school my parents chose for me was called Cressbrook in the pretty town of Kirkby Lonsdale about ten miles from Sedbergh.

The headmaster was an intimidating man called David Donald, known universally as D.A.D. He was a father figure to the seventy or so boys in his charge, but one from the Old Testament. Or Sparta. Had the law of the land allowed it, I believe that he would have had all the new boys left on top of an icy fell all night to see who survived and could go on to be a warrior like him. An old Sedberghian himself, an Oxford graduate and a decorated fighter pilot, he had played a distinguished role in the Battle of Britain until shot down. He was stern; a hard but fair man, usually restrained but occasionally given to fits of bad temper. Later one of the teachers explained to us that this could be ascribed to the fact that his legs were full of shrapnel that moved around from time to time causing him agony. Later still we met someone who had served with him in the RAF. Apparently, he was much admired and respected (if not liked) because he was a brave pilot with an unfortunate penchant for early morning runs, cold baths and porridge. Good mood or bad, both staff and pupils at Cressbrook were in awe of him. Probably most parents were too. He seldom raised his voice but he had an aura about him that discouraged any form of familiarity. He was surprisingly gentle with boys who were not fit, such as those who were asthmatic or overweight. But with boys who were merely lazy he could be harsh, pushing them well beyond their normal limits. At Cressbrook you were supposed to carry your shield back from the battle or else be carried home lying dead on it.

There was no chance of stepping out of line with D.A.D. He was strongly supported by his wife. I never knew her first name but she was known by the boys, and possibly some of the staff, as the Dragon. The reasons for this became evident within minutes of meeting her. Cressbrook was a school of the strength- through-joy variety. Given that the boys were aged between eight and thirteen, it was an even tougher institution than Sedbergh, its more celebrated neighbour up the road, which to the extent it was famous for anything, was notorious for its physical toughness.

D.A.D. believed in rigorous academic training, but he also believed that a rounded education should include physical exercise. Lots of it. In fact, we often felt that we were students in an Ancient Greek gymnasium or that we were novices at the Shaolin monastery. But instead of the martial arts, we spent the time on rugby and soccer in the winter, cricket, athletics and swimming in the summer, fell running and hiking all year round.

The day began at 7 am with a cold bath (total immersion mandatory) or a length of the outdoor pool in the summer. A brisk walk of a mile or so followed before morning prayers. Then there were classes until 6 pm but with two or three hours set aside for vigorous physical exercise seven days a week. That was a typical day.

In fact, D.A.D. never missed an opportunity to be outdoors. In the summer, if we were fortunate enough to have one of those rare days when it was hot and sunny in Cumbria, the rumours would start during the morning break that there would be an announcement at lunchtime. Sometimes they had substance. At the end of lunch D.A.D. would stand, say grace and declare a half-holiday exhorting us to behave ourselves and to be polite to those we met. And that was the only rule. For the rest of the day seventy boys were allowed to run free, roaming the countryside going wherever we liked. We were entirely unsupervised.

Given the number of lakes, rivers, tarns, slurry pits, cliffs, barbed wire and other ways that boys could harm themselves, it was an act of extraordinary courage on his part. To the best of my knowledge it was never abused or led to an accident. In some ways Cressbrook was traditional, but in others it was well ahead of its time.

D.A.D. had an idiosyncratic sense of fun. He celebrated his 50th birthday by taking the whole school, every one of us, plus a number of teachers who had 'volunteered', to climb Helvellyn, one of the higher mountains in the Lake District, with a potentially dangerous section called Striding Edge. So far so good. However, we climbed it in the middle of a blizzard and with almost zero visibility. Since we were lightly dressed in gym shorts, T-shirts, a light anorak and plimsolls that were totally unsuited to climbing mountains in even bright sunshine it was a minor miracle that no-one succumbed to exposure or wandered off into the blizzard never to be seen again. But D.A.D. held a roll call at the summit and he counted us all again at the base. And then, once he was sure that we were all safe, off he went again striding back to the coaches in the car park, utterly unrepentant, his kilt swirling around his shrapnel filled legs. And if I remember correctly we did at least have a special dinner that evening and a birthday cake (and spent the next few days rubbing zinc ointment into severely chapped legs). We sang, 'Happy Birthday,' with genuine feeling because when all was said and done, Cressbrook felt like a family, albeit one ruled over by a tough warrior of a man.

In the depths of winter (and how could one forget the big freeze of 1962-63) it became a matter of pride to see who could reach a bath first in the morning and have the privilege of breaking the ice that had formed overnight. D.A.D. personally supervised the exercise and anyone who he considered had not immersed himself or spent long enough in the bath had to get back in again.

I suspect that nowadays, D.A.D.'s all weather mountain climbing exploits and his means of waking up his young charges would almost certainly result in his prosecution and the closure of the school. Within a few years the liberal use of beating by slipper or cane (painful and agonising respectively) would be outlawed. But in the early to mid-1960s we danced to a different tune and I never thought of him or heard D.A.D. described as cruel or sadistic. If you wanted tough love for your children, and an iron fist in an iron glove, Cressbrook was the place to send them. Harsh though the regime at Cressbrook may seem by modern standards, I was very happy there overall and it played an important and positive role in my development. Two events, one right at the beginning, the other right at the end, illustrate how far I had come.

On the first day of my first term my parents drove me up to Kirkby Lonsdale along what became a very familiar route for the next ten years. I was in good spirits as we drove first to Halifax, and then onto Skipton. But as we approached Settle the atmosphere in the car became tense. I became quiet as anxiety about my new life started to dawn on me. As we drove across Clapham Common (North Yorkshire), past a wonderful watering hole that we would come to love, the Goat Gap Farm, I started to feel nervous. My parents said little but I knew they too felt apprehensive.

Being obsessed with punctuality, as we always were, we turned up at the school before any other parents arrived with their offspring.

D.A.D. came out to meet us and helped my father unload my school trunk from the car. They then had a brief conversation in which he reassured them that all would be well. It was then time to say goodbye.

My mother hugged me and told me that she would write to me every week and that she was sure I would be fine. I could see she was on the verge of tears and I felt a lump in my throat.

My father also looked tense but ever the Broadbent, and ever the army officer, he said rather stiffly that they would come and see me in a few weeks but urged me meanwhile to work hard, play hard and to make friends.

Then they were gone and I, a basically happy but rather reserved boy of eight, stood in the driveway and looked after them.

D.A.D said that he had some work to do, but that other boys, including new boys would arrive soon. He suggested, not unkindly, that I spend the intervening time exploring and getting to know my new surroundings. He then disappeared inside the house.

Now I was completely alone. Cautiously (taking care that I could still see the spot where I was standing at the moment my parents departed) I went in one direction to look at the big garden with its monkey puzzle and cedar trees, then in another and then back to the spot to which I was invisibly chained. This was not Oakscar.

I then decided I should go and look round the big rambling house with its several staircases and dormitories and lots of doors that only seemed to lead to more doors and more staircases. And that was my mistake.

I set off to take a look around and within minutes I was totally lost.

Suddenly, I was seized by panic. I tried to get out of the house, but the harder I tried the more lost I became. I started to cry.

By the time I was discovered – probably half an hour later, although it felt like several days – I was sobbing uncontrollably. At one point I was almost hysterical and oblivious to various attempts to console me.

I carried on crying all day and was still in floods of tears that evening.

D.A.D. looked at me sharply and then, in front of the whole school, said in a cold voice utterly devoid of sympathy, 'Stop that, immediately,' thereby adding complete humiliation in front of the entire school to my list of woes. With difficulty I did as I was told and brought myself under control. For a time.

But at bedtime the matron came round to see that all was as it should be. She noticed that I had brought my favourite teddy bear from home and, despite my protests, she confiscated him.

I cried again and she said, 'Stop crying, big boys don't cry.' At the time the irony was lost on me.

I cried myself to sleep, but when I woke up the next morning I did not cry. Nor did I do so until the night my father died almost forty years later.

Several years after my father's death (my mother died three years after him, having endured a ghastly period of inconsolable widowhood), I happened to be on holiday in Australia where I met my wife Joyce's brother Winston, one of the country's leading psychiatrists.

I am not sure how it came about, but I found myself ignoring my own best advice... Never discuss anything personal with a psychiatrist; you tell them you have a problem and they say, 'No you haven't, you have a dozen more.'

We exchanged stories about our childhoods, and I described the trauma of my arrival at Cressbrook. 'It was odd,' I said. 'None of the other new boys behaved like that, although quite a few of us must have been feeling pretty sorry for ourselves. But I was so distraught that, as I discovered later, D.A.D. had called my parents and discussed the possibility that I might need to be taken away from the school. I still feel ashamed and embarrassed when I think about it.'

'There is nothing odd at all about your behaviour, and no need to feel ashamed or embarrassed,' Winston replied. 'For the second time in your life you had just been abandoned and betrayed. The primal wound had just split open again. Your adoption had resulted in a terrible mistake. There is no need to feel bad. Your parents may have been wonderful people who loved you dearly, but what they did to you was extraordinarily cruel. You were eight years old and had just been abandoned again.'

At the time he said it, I thought what fanciful nonsense, but as things were to turn out later I came to believe that he had seen what had eluded everyone else. There really was a powerful connection.

The second event: it is summer 1967. I have just turned thirteen. I am over six feet tall and slim but surprisingly strong. My voice broke almost two years ago. My ability to hit top C in Kirkby Lonsdale parish church seems to have belonged to another person in a different age. My singing voice now sounds like a Yorkshire version of Lee Marvin.

I am in my last term at Cressbrook, having been accepted by Sedbergh School, for which the prep school was an unofficial feeder. This is of itself no great achievement. We used to joke that you were only sent to Sedbergh if you had escaped from two other camps. In fact, it was settled by an interview and a reasonable performance in the Common Entrance exam. However, someone at Sedbergh made a serious

110

blunder when they failed one Cressbrook boy due to a poor result. His name was William Blackledge Beaumont – future England rugby captain, British and Irish Lions and ultimately the number one figure in world rugby.

My good friend Rick Fisher and I had been over to Sedbergh to sit the scholarship exam. Neither of us had been successful in winning a scholarship, which would have helped financially, but both of us had been given places at the school. My English paper and an impressive interview (during which, oddly, we had discussed George Bernard Shaw's *Saint Joan* and the Holocaust) had been enough to secure my place; Rick's excellence in Maths saw him home.

I have been at Cressbrook for almost five years, and although I still struggle with Maths I have made good progress academically in a school with decent standards of teaching in most subjects. I have shown my sporting ability on the rugby field where I have become an influential player; I have grown taller and stronger than anyone else in our school or any of the schools we play. If I can maintain the gap between myself and others in my age group for another five years I am going to be a force to be reckoned with. I do not have good hand to eye coordination and to my disappointment I will never excel at cricket or squash, fives or golf for that matter. However, my height, strength and speed, and my willingness to lie face down in the mud while being trampled on by a dozen other boys can be deployed to good effect on a rugby pitch. From the beginning I have discovered a passion for the game. We win every match under my captaincy and my parents say that watching me hand off would-be tacklers is like watching a man against boys.

D.A.D., who I felt was always a little suspicious of me, has recognised that I have leadership qualities and has also made me Head of School.

I allow myself to daydream... Following in the footsteps of other old Cressbrookians, Bill Beaumont, with whom I was quite friendly at one time, and also John Spencer, who went on to play for England in a short-lived but glamorous centre pairing with the great David Duckham, is it possible that I too...? Surely not.

But Cressbrook has been good for me; it has given me back my self-confidence after the mauling it had received at the hands of Mrs Wright, it has brought me out of myself. I had been slightly introverted or at least reflective. Cressbrook has brought me out of my shell and made me, though not exactly extrovert, more assertive. It has taught me what I am good at and what I am not so good at. D.A.D. has seen in me a talent for leadership. Cressbrook has taught me to be self-reliant and to keep calm under pressure.

It is school sports day. In the past I have not particularly enjoyed this because there have always been boys who could run faster or jump further. But while everyone has seen me grow much taller, they may not have observed how much bigger and stronger I have become in the past year.

So we come to the first event, the 100 yards, and here I am pitted against the one boy in the school who does not like me. I don't know why but I do not care for him either. It's a chemistry thing. The starter's pistol goes and the two of us are out of the blocks fast. We are dead level at 25 yards but half way down the track suddenly I cannot see him. I run like hell and somewhat to my surprise I win comfortably. It turns out that he has torn his hamstring and collapsed in agony. I am indecently happy about this, especially when I am told that I have set a new school record, which is still standing when Cressbrook School closes (following D.A.D.'s retirement some fifteen years later).

Then it is on to the high jump. Here I hit a problem because on my second jump I land awkwardly and hurt my arm badly. I think I must have broken it. Later, X-rays will confirm a fracture. So, I pull out of the rest of the event (I still come second) and Dr Morris, the school doctor, who is attending the event as a parent and just in case, drives me down the hill to his surgery. He also thinks my arm is broken and, while he bandages me and puts it in a sling, I tell him what I want to do.

'Are you quite sure?' he asks and I nod vigorously. And he is a good sport so we race back up the hill and we are just in time for Dr Morris to have a word with D.A.D.

The headmaster walks over to me and says rather sharply, 'Are you quite sure you want to do this?'

I say, 'Yes Sir.' And for once D.A.D., hard man that he is, looks worried.

He thinks for a moment and then says, 'Very well, but if the pain is too great you stop, is that understood?'

I say, 'Yes sir, thank you.'

So, to widespread surprise and audible murmuring amongst the crowd of several hundred, I take my place in the final of the 400 yards race. My main rival is my good friend Rick Fisher. And I have barely secured permission to race than we start. After 200 yards he has a clear lead. No one else is in sight and I am struggling and my arm is hurting like hell. After 300 it looks as though Rick has the race sewn up because it is just too hard to run with one arm. But from somewhere deep inside me I feel a kind of fury and it drives me forward. I no longer care about pain or anything else. I close in on Rick and as we come off the final bend I draw level with him and then, buoyed by the roars of several hundred people (for this is a big day for boys, parents and the town), I find the extra gear, ease past him and breast the finishing tape three yards ahead. The applause is tumultuous.

My father, who has come up for the day, looks overwhelmed and D.A.D. smiles at me from a distance and nods in silent approval. It is by some way the best day of my life.

I did not know it then, but my triumph at Cressbrook was to be the last time I ever really shone as an individual in my entire sporting career.

Chapter 5 - Dura Virum Nutrix

In the autumn of 1967, I travelled back in time several decades and found myself living in a Victorian institution with Victorian values. That is to say, I started at Sedbergh School. It was familiar territory in many ways because the two schools were only ten miles apart and one was an unofficial prep school for the other. The links were strong. D.A.D. was an old Sedberghian and a great supporter. We used to go and watch the Sedbergh First XV play home rugby matches and our heroes were people like John Spencer who had been at Cressbrook. John would go on to play for Cambridge University, England and the British and Irish Lions. I was also a member of the part of the choir supplied by Cressbrook for a performance of the *Messiah* arranged by the school; despite its reputation for philistinism, Sedbergh was strong musically. I was therefore acquainted with certain aspects of the school and knew what to expect.

Nevertheless, having been at the top of a very small hill, it required quite an adjustment to start again at the foot of a mountain. Within a fortnight I had quietly shelved any aspirations I might have had of making a name for myself as a sportsman.

Sedbergh School had been revered by several generations of Broadbents and it was part of the tradition that the boys in the family were all sent there; my father went to Sedbergh as did all his brothers, his father and his grandfather too. My cousin Hugh had been there a year when I arrived and his younger brother Andy would join us two years later. My father put my name down for the school when I was three months old. I grew up thinking it was one of the great schools of England. It was only later that I learned, to my disappointment, that although it was respected in the north of England, hardly anyone in the south had ever heard of it. Compared with the great names of English education like Winchester and Eton it was second division, and small too, with a maximum number of 450 boys. At the time of the Great War, Sedbergh had about 300 boys. That 257 old Sedberghians were killed in the War, three of them winning the Victoria Cross, gives an idea of the type of man it looked to produce.

Sedbergh offered a certain type of education that some people admired and some did not. The school motto was 'dura virum nutrix' which translated as 'hard nurse of men' and it was no vacuous slogan. On a sunny afternoon, standing at one end of a huge strip of grass, half of which was dedicated to one of the most beautiful cricket pitches in England, it was easy to think of this setting as an idyllic place to grow up. But ploughing through the mud of a sodden rugby pitch or running across the fells in the sleet and wind of a Cumbrian February told a different story. Sedbergh was a school that believed in

118

the big outdoors and made no concessions at all to the appalling weather that is a feature of that part of the country.

For some people the relentless insistence on rugby and on the outdoor life was liberating and they took every opportunity that was on offer. One of the lifelong friends I made there, John Moore, was typical of this group. Day after day, week after week he would come back to the house soaked through and half frozen from rugby or caving or canoeing or climbing or fishing. In his spare time he did a little work and breezed into Cambridge with an ease that depressed drones like me.

Others, equally able-bodied but missing the creature comforts of home and resentful of the obsession with rugby and the school's scornful attitude to other sports, especially football, were much less enthusiastic. Another great friend, Glen Cocker, now retired after a successful career in the Crown Prosecution Service, would have thrived at a school that offered the choice and the opportunity to develop his considerable footballing skills. He would also have appreciated being in a school that just occasionally admitted that the weather really was too bad for games. At Sedbergh there was no choice: march or die.

My own position was somewhere in between. I still enjoyed the rugby even after scaling down my ambitions to realistic levels. I loved the matches against other houses because of the fanatical commitment they generated and the chance to play on the same team as your closest friends. I also had three years on the school first XV and ended up as captain, although I was nowhere near as talented as many of my illustrious predecessors, nor my distinguished successors.

My quarrel with Sedbergh was not the amount of time we were obliged to spend outside; it was with the quality of teaching inside the classroom. If you examined the staff list at that time, superficially it might look impressive. Almost all the teaching staff had degrees from Oxford or Cambridge. But if one had dug a little deeper it might have become evident that they were mostly third class honours. Furthermore, very few of them had any teacher training, or indeed any other experience beyond teaching. They were, in a sense, perpetual schoolboys, living in an isolated community, and largely ignorant of the wider world. As the school song said, with unintentional irony, it was the hills that stood around them that made the Sedbergh man. The masters might or might not know their subject, but could they pass on their knowledge and inspire their pupils? That was a very different question.

I began to see the staff as a motley crew who had ended up in, rather than actively choosing, Sedbergh, which despite the town's later pretensions to become a centre for books, was hardly in the mainstream of culture. In fact, unless one had an inordinate love of countryside, Sedbergh was a backwater and the staff were refugees of one sort or another. They were caricatures of themselves and I cannot now think of the occasional glimpse of the masters' common room without thinking of the dive bar scene in George Lucas' film *Star Wars*. Considering my parents were beggaring themselves to send me there, I felt strongly that we deserved better. There were one or two notable exceptions and it was my good fortune that one of them was my English teacher, a Welshman who had been to Cambridge and had almost played rugby for Wales (he was the great Cliff Morgan's understudy). Most people who have done well academically usually remember one teacher who was a particular inspiration. Alan Barter was mine. But as to the rest, they were at best mediocre, and so I protested.

In part, my 'protest' was nothing more than the mischievous tendency of many adolescent boys. I would almost certainly have misbehaved wherever I had gone to school. Nevertheless, for a period of about two years I was well and truly off the rails. Boys will be boys, but I suspect that my delinquency and my relentless pursuit of illicit pleasures was a signal of a much more profound discontent.

Whenever I, and a few like-minded souls, could find the opportunity, we would make a dash for the nearest watering holes. The pubs in the town were considered off limits because they were patronised by the masters and we were determined to have our pleasures and not get caught. The village of Dent a few miles away and the Railway Inn on the road to Kirkby Lonsdale were favoured destinations. There we would drink beer rapidly for two or three hours and smoke ourselves silly on French cigarettes, smuggled in at the beginning of term. Then we would buy a bottle of whisky to sustain us on the return journey and stumble back just in time for dinner and the evening roll call. And on Field Days, which were open days, we had a field day.

This flouting of the strict school rules went on for about two years. We took enormous risks. Discovery would have resulted in immediate expulsion (bringing untold shame on the House of Broadbent). But while we were almost certainly suspected, we were never caught. This remarkable record owed more to our ability to execute rather than to formulate any strategic plan – the scaling of high walls at speed while paralytic with alcohol being a hallmark of this fluid_and nameless group of reprobates.

The day came for this amorphous group to disband, or rather to melt into the civilian population. It evaporated into thin air when several members of the club that did not exist, were seen 'fraternising' (I use the term loosely) with local girls. The staff and the housemaster of the suspects went into a huddle with the headmaster. This was followed by further meetings in which the suspects' parents were invited to call on the headmaster for a cup of tea and a raised eyebrow. This might have led to a number of boys seeking alternative institutions to complete their education, had it not been for one sensible, far-sighted father (perhaps drawing on his own past). He pointed out that although such activities might run counter to the ethos of the school, no law had been broken and that it was inevitable that it would happen from time to time here. Elsewhere, on a different planet to the school, it was known as human nature.

When it came to my turn to be interrogated by the headmaster, I put up a spirited defence of the laws governing human behaviour and what I considered to be a natural justice. I agreed that caning would be inappropriate (and could be seen in this context as a form of sexual perversion). I then made the only comment that really angered him. I said that it was time for Sedbergh to consider going coeducational. 'Out of the question,' he snapped irritably. 'You clearly haven't grasped what this school stands for.'

I replied, 'With respect sir, I believe I have.' I didn't have the courage to add, 'and that is precisely what is wrong with it.'

As to my parents, they almost never mentioned 'the incident' but I was quite surprised when my mother once made reference to it. She said, 'You know that D.A.D. talked about your adoption with us, and warned Sedbergh in advance of

123

your arrival that you had great ability but that you had a very dark side and that it would one day surface.'

After my O levels were navigated successfully I gave up my vices and increasingly channelled my energies, thereby achieving a measure of redemption. However, at the end of my last summer term I was 'invited' to go and see the headmaster again, which usually spelt trouble. I went with some trepidation to his house. Canings were always administered in his office, which offered some small comfort.

He began quite gently, saying that an issue had arisen on which he sought my view. 'We have to decide who the captain of the First XV is going to be next term,' he said. 'And here is our dilemma; you will be the senior player in the side and in normal circumstances you would be the automatic choice. You are a good rugby player but not an exceptional one by the standards of this school (which had produced by then almost thirty internationals). You have leadership qualities and a natural authority. My problem is that you always seem to lead people in the wrong direction. Can you assure me that if you would captain what is a young side, you will be a credit to yourself and the school, particularly on away games when visiting schools which are less disciplined than ours?'

I assured him that I could and would. As things turned out I made a pretty good fist of it and the young team I left at Christmas 1972 would go on to achieve great things.

I had the satisfaction of knowing that by combining the two greatest honours a Sedbergh boy could aspire to – Captain of the First XV and an Open Scholarship to Cambridge (and certainly in that order), I became the most successful Broadbent ever to attend the school. Given that I was almost certainly also the worst behaved, there was more than a hint of irony in this.

Words words words.

I was born with a talent for words. No. Let me stop there. It would be less elegant, but more precise, to say that from a very early age, I exhibited an interest in words and that this developed into a verbal dexterity that was above average. It was certainly well ahead of any other aptitude I might have shown, cognitive or physical. Had it been matched by an equally strong imagination or creative capacity I would have said I had a talent. Sadly, it wasn't and any thoughts I might have had about becoming, say, a successful novelist, disappeared almost as soon as they had forced their way into my mind and begun to mock me. Even now, in my premature dotage, I sometimes look at a book cover of a novel by John Le Carré or Robert Harris, see the author's photograph on the jacket and think, just for a second, that could be me.

It could not, of course. In that respect, I am no different from hundreds, no, thousands of would be authors. And amongst them only a tiny fraction will ever get published and of that fraction only a tiny number will ever make a living, much less a lavish one. The same is true of poets, actors, painters, architects and musicians. Even bestselling authors are advised, 'Don't give up the day job just yet.'

Nevertheless, I discovered an immense appetite for books, long before completing the obligatory Enid Blyton, Beatrix Potter, A. A. Milne apprenticeship. I wish I had discovered Michael Morpurgo at that age, but he became well known much later. At a very early age I devoured the works of Arthur Conan Doyle and C. S. Lewis, choosing them simply because they were in the house. I then diversified and absorbed, open-mouthed, a wonderful book called *The Readers Digest Junior Treasury*, an excellent starting point for any young person showing an interest in reading. I particularly enjoyed the stories about Jim Corbett, the big game hunter, and Ernest Shackleton, the explorer. Then it was on to Agatha Christie. I also read all the James Bond oeuvre, having found it in a trunk in the loft in what was one the most exciting discoveries of my life.

There was another epiphany. One of the most vivid memories of my entire life is sitting on the beach of Portreath in north Cornwall in early September 1963, sheltering behind a small canvas screen from the freezing wind which blew in all year from the Atlantic. I was spellbound by John Le Carré's

126

The Spy Who Came In from the Cold, which had just been published, I was enthralled by this wondrous object that could take you wherever you wanted to go. Not only were the words providing an alternative reality, they were blocking out everything else.

Until that moment I had not considered the book as an object deserving of such veneration, but my time on the beach was a Damascene moment and for next fifty years I would always have one to hand. I was hooked.

An indiscriminate looting and consumption of every book in the house followed my early incursion into Le Carré's riveting portrayal of this secret world. This meant working my way through John Buchan, C. S. Forester and Tolkien's *The Hobbit* (I saved the big one for later). By the end of six months, I had read every book in the house of any interest whatsoever. My parents were both avid readers but their tastes were middlebrow, and they made extensive use of the excellent local library, so there was not an unlimited choice.

Pompously, at the age of twelve, I attempted to draw a line between Literature with a capital L on the one hand and reading for pleasure on the other. The books my parents read clearly belonged to the second category. Inevitably at that age I drew a straight line and with a childish simplicity determined to stay on the right side of it and not waste time on frivolity. In reality the line is never straight and shifts constantly. John Le

Carré is now taught at Cambridge. Will Robert Harris' *An Officer and a Spy* be included in the Literature category and if not why not? Was Dickens a great novelist or the tireless producer of pulp fiction to tight deadlines?

As for my own writing, I was producing essays at the age of twelve that would have been a credit to an eighteen year old.

At Sedbergh, when I was fourteen, my English teacher bravely declined to mark my work any longer because he said it was so much better than anything he could produce. He felt it should be judged by a more senior colleague. He was brave and he was right.

Year after year, as soon as I was eligible, I won the school prizes for English and History at both Cressbrook and at Sedbergh, except one year when I lost out to my good friend Nick Minns on the senior History prize. I was mortified by this failure but came back strongly to reclaim it the next year and to take the Divinity prize as well. Seldom can the latter have been awarded to a less deserving student.

Had I gone to school at, say Winchester, I like to think that I would still probably have come top – maybe not – but the gap between me and the next guy might have been close. At Sedbergh I was in a class of my own and although my English teacher Alan Barter, who was excellent, was proud of me, some of his colleagues viewed me with a degree of suspicion.

Nick applied to read History at Cambridge but his teacher was a drunk and he failed the entrance exam which, given his intellect, was a travesty.

Some members of staff thought of me as an aspiring intellectual; it was not a compliment. My only redeeming quality was that I played rugby as well.

At the age of sixteen I took my O levels and passed all that were considered essential, as well as some that were not. As soon as I was able to jettison the subjects that I disliked (what on earth was Physics about?) and concentrate on those I was good at, my performance rocketed. As an aside, it is interesting to note as an aspect of human development that neither of the boys who were awarded the top scholarships in the year I applied went on to enjoy further academic success, nor, as far as I know, did they have particularly distinguished careers. In this respect their intellectual development was like my sporting career. It peaked at the age of thirteen and then stalled.

And so my triumphant progress continued – for a while. On the strength of my A level results (straight As and two grade one S levels a foregone conclusion and barely worth a mention) I was invited to Jesus College, Cambridge at the beginning of the academic year in October 1972. I had selected it after a five-minute discussion with my mentors at Sedbergh, firstly because my dear friend John Moore had won a place there and would be going up a year before me, secondly my English master, a Welshman, pointed out that the leading English literature critic and fellow Welshman, Raymond Williams, was also a Fellow there and was supported by other talented scholars (what a huge understatement that turned out to be!) Finally, it is the only Cambridge college with its rugby pitch in its own grounds. With a hat trick like this I looked for no further assurances and set off to win my place.

At this point I suffered a rare setback. After extremely friendly and positive meetings with Bruce Sparkes, the admissions gatekeeper, and Robin Donkin, who was to play the role of supportive godfather, I had a lengthy interview with Howard Erskine Hill. If I were given a place, he would be my director of studies. Unfortunately the chemistry between us was poor. Howard, a little mouse of a man and a world authority on Alexander Pope, was so shy that he made me nervous. I think that he looked at this strapping young man with a distinctly unascetic, unintellectual face and manner and thought he smelled a public school stereotype whose intellectual limitations had been plastered over with an expensive private education. Making matters worse, when he asked me to name a couple of works I would like to discuss, instead of playing straight down the fairway with, say, *Tess of the D'Urbervilles* and *Othello,* about which I could have held my own with any academic in the world, I had a senior moment at the age of eighteen and nominated James Joyce and Samuel Richardson, neither of whom I knew well. It would have been better if I said I enjoyed books about football or submarines. I knew by the end of a very difficult one-hour inquisition that I had not put my best foot forward.

Sure enough a few days after my return to Sedbergh the message arrived: 'Broadbent is a possibility but we would like to reserve judgement until we have seen the results of his entrance exam.'

I was mortified but consoled by the two masters who ran the First XV that such things happen.

I responded in the way I did in those days. I simply redoubled my efforts and vented my fury with myself with some spirited displays on the rugby field. And I had my revenge.

I felt in good form when sitting the entrance exam. In due course a telegram arrived from Bruce Sparkes and although it was 44 years ago I remember it almost verbatim. It said, 'Congratulations, your performance was outstanding. The best of anyone in the Group (of eight colleges of which Jesus was one for adjudication) you have been awarded an Open Scholarship. We look forward to welcoming you to the College next October, best wishes B J Sparkes, Admissions tutor'.

I don't think I have ever received a more welcome message in my life. Mum cried and Dad, who was at home recovering from his second heart attack and facing early retirement, tried unsuccessfully to cover his emotions by reaching for the gin bottle. It wasn't that I had got into Cambridge – most of the Broadbents went to Oxford or Cambridge – and it had been taken for granted since I was thirteen that I would go (how arrogant can you get), it was the manner in which I did it which stunned my parents. It certainly took me by surprise. I knew I was good but I didn't think I was that good. All my parents knew up to that point was that they had a son who, for the last couple of years, had come home for holidays, said a perfunctory hello and went up to his room and stayed there, reading and reading until it was time to go back to school. I must have been one of only a handful of children in England whose parents begged them to stop studying. They feared for my health at one stage, though they need not have worried. I was blissfully content doing what I enjoyed most. It was a triumph.

After a very happy Christmas that year I had nine months in which to find something useful to do. Here I had an immense stroke of good fortune stemming from a conversation with John Moore's father, who was at that time the chief executive of the Sheffield steel company Spear and Jackson. He said they could find some work for a French speaking person to spend time in Paris doing market research and asked me if I would like the job. I almost bit his arm off in my haste to accept.

As a result, while Nick Minns went to work as a petrol pump attendant in his hometown of Berkhamsted, I was sent to Paris after a few days in Sheffield being briefed by one of the management consultants working for the company and now charged with providing my minder. I set off for France accompanied by John Moore. We caught the ferry from Dover and the train to Paris.

At that time I had been abroad twice, once to Spain and once to Germany. I had no idea how much travel I would do later and this trip with John was very exciting. Paris! After ten years in dour boarding schools in Cumbria, it offered some real opportunities for fun.

We got off to a solid start. We stayed for a couple of days at a pleasant hotel on the Boulevard des Italiens. We toured parts of the city and when we tired of that we went to the cinema and watched Pasolini's *Il Decameron*. We also spent some time in the Latin Quarter watching the hated CRS police chasing protesting students through the narrow streets. It looked like a reprise of 1968.

Then it was time for John to go back to England and to begin another term at Cambridge. Before he left we met the company's agent in Paris over lunch in the Latin Quarter. I sketched out what I thought was an appropriate programme for the next few months, starting with desk research in Paris and later, field research in Paris, Lyon, Marseille and other centres.

M. Laurent listened, nodded from time to time at me and then, true Parisian that he was, he said that he thought the plan was sensible but that my French was execrable and needed to improve, and that he would recommend a short, intensive course at the Alliance Française.

I felt somewhat crestfallen by his assessment of my language skills (I did have an A grade A level which surely counted for something).

He found me a small hotel near the Château de Vincennes and asked me to wait until he contacted me again, when I would be given a green light to proceed, or other instructions. Which I did.

I waited and waited for almost six weeks. I tried to reach M. Laurent many times but I could never get hold of him.

Meanwhile, I started to read, working my way through a list that the college had sent with the suggestion that I select titles that interested me. I had brought several books with me in those pre-Kindle days and I bought several more at Shakespeare and Company, one of the great institutions of the Left Bank made famous by the Lost Generation of writers in the 1920s.

The winter of 1972/73 was bitterly cold. I stayed in the hotel room most of the time and by the end of it I was bored with my room, running low on funds and frankly disillusioned with Paris and with Spear and Jackson and the project.

I was ready to go home.

However, just at the moment I was about to give up, George Moore himself arrived in Paris with a senior management consultant called Don Fisk. After a private discussion with M. Laurent (which I suspected was not entirely to the latter's liking), George Moore apologised profusely, said there had been a misunderstanding and that everything had now been sorted out. They then took me out to dinner at their hotel, the Plaza Athénée, which made me feel better and then to the Crazy Horse, which made me feel better still. They said that I should begin work immediately, that my plan was excellent but that I might benefit from polishing up my French – which may or may not have been just a sop to humour M. Laurent. They also said that Laurent would set up a bank account for me, that my (small) salary, backdated to the day I started in Sheffield, would be paid into it and he would give me a generous expense float for travel et cetera. Don Fisk assured me that one of his consultants would be over once a month to review progress.

The next day they were gone off to inspect another part of the Spear and Jackson expansion in Europe. But everything they said would happen did happen and I really began to enjoy Paris and the little job I had been tasked with.

I started my project by going to see the commercial attaché at the British Embassy. He was extremely helpful in digging out all kinds of published statistics on the French market for steel products, as well articles about the French attitude to foreign goods and particularly, in the case of Parisians, their fondness for 'maisons secondaires'. I was thus able to satisfy my masters in Sheffield and retain my sense of being useful.

I dutifully attended my classes at the Alliance Française and improved my language skills a little. However, I never really mastered the language because I did not work hard enough and because I found many Parisians met foreigners' attempts to address them in their own language with thinly veiled contempt. Overall, in my dealings with Parisians I found them to be unapproachable and frequently downright rude. In fairness, in recent trips to the city I have found most of them to be transformed – polite, courteous and unfailingly helpful. I have no idea why this welcome improvement occurred, but at the time I lived there it was the one aspect of the city that I found disappointing. In other respects, life in Paris in 1973 was idyllic.

Working one day at the Embassy I happened to see a notice board inviting readers to join the British Rugby Club of Paris. Here was a language I spoke fluently and I lost no time in making a telephone call and in responding to an invitation to go to no. 5 rue Daunou, which was and still is the unofficial headquarters of the BRCP. From that moment on I never wanted for company or friends. The Club provided a very active social life for the rest of my time in France. They had a relaxed attitude to physical fitness, especially when compared with Sedbergh, and took little interest in the tedious business of training. Although we did book a session in a gym once a week, which the fanatics like me attended, the heavy demands on international lawyers, accountants and architects made collective training sessions difficult.

I was sad to leave Paris but the project came to an end and I became surplus to requirements. It was time to get on with the next stage. My research findings were subsumed into a larger report on Spear and Jackson's business plans for continental Europe. I have no idea how much attention anyone paid to them. Nevertheless, I have experienced childish pleasure every time I have seen the company's products, stocked in the numerous department and hardware stores I have made a point of visiting during several trips to France since my first job experience.

Chapter 6 - Cambridge

In the course of my life, I have encountered only two great institutions with towering reputations that they fully deserved. One of them lay in my future, the other was here and now.

It had been my intention to go Cambridge University since I was about thirteen and just starting at Sedbergh (possibly earlier) and I had never considered the possibility that I might not be accepted. Given the number of intelligent and able people who would also like to go to Cambridge, but for one reason or another do not do so, this was extraordinarily presumptuous. Nevertheless, it was how I thought.

Although the family had a marked bias for Oxford and I had been born there, I never considered it an option. It was Cambridge or nowhere for me (though for the sake of good order I also accepted a provisional place at Sussex).

I thought I would get into Cambridge but my position at the top of the tree had surprised me and probably surprised others too. After the experience of moving from primary school to Cressbrook, and then from the prep school to Sedbergh, I was braced for another big step up, but the height of the step when it came still took my breath away.

Jesus College stands just outside and slightly to the north east of the city centre. It is not one of the oldest colleges nor one of the grandest but it is in my biased view one of the most beautiful. Like the other colleges it is constructed around several large courtyards – for example Chapel Court, West and North Court. The buildings are constructed with numerous staircases immediately accessible from the courtyards leading to rooms or sets of rooms occupied by the fellows and other high officials (the Manciple and the Praelector being two of the more obscure). The majority of the rooms are occupied by graduate and undergraduate students. A board at the entrance to each staircase lists the names of the occupants of the rooms.

There are parallels with some of the country's public schools but Jesus College is far more beautiful than any school I have ever seen. The College is set in its own magnificent grounds with ample room for a rugby pitch, a football pitch and a cricket pitch in summer. It has a fine library, a lovely chapel, a proud tradition in rowing and a superb English department. It was marvellous to see on one of the staircases the name Prof. R. Williams, something of a cult figure in the 1960s and 1970s. One would often meet the great man striding down the Chimney, the path into the College bordered by high walls. I did go and see Raymond Williams on one occasion, but as he seemed distracted and bored with our conversation I did not stay long. I retreated, reflecting that while teaching undergraduates is required from all fellows, research, writing and being published were far more important to most of them. Undergraduates were a distraction.

How could you not feel inspired by such a wonderful setting? How could you not feel privileged to study when surrounded by world-class intellects? Oxford and Cambridge are often said by their detractors to be for the privileged elite; a remnant of a bygone age. It was indeed a privilege to be able to spend three years studying the best that has been thought and said. Without hindrance. It was a privilege to live in, and have access to, such a centre of excellence. It was a privilege to be taught by the most brilliant minds of the day, people who could think things that you would never have thought of yourself. It was a privilege to have such talented fellow students with whom to debate and compete. But, make no mistake, these were hard earned privileges. We knew that we were some of the brightest young people in the country – an elite but not a club for the progeny of the rich industrialist or the lord of the manor.

It is probably true to say that Jesus College was more advanced than most on the question of social mobility and did all it could to build up a reputation for fairness. If you applied to Jesus and were bright enough you were in; no one sat up at night putting crosses against the applications of what might be referred to as 'working class' boys. You could be the son of a

Malaysian business tycoon or a nephew of the Queen, or the son of a stevedore or a plumber. Or the son of the managing director of a declining mill in Huddersfield.

In the year I matriculated, for example, there were about ten of us reading English. I was the only one to have been to public school. I do not believe that it was ever an issue, except that few students of English also liked rough games. I believe the same was true for other subjects. The only advantages that it conferred on me were that having grown up in a literate, educated, middle class household, I had probably enjoyed more access to books and was therefore better read than some. Also, I was used to institutional life in old buildings that might have intimidated someone from a different background and fitted easily into a new and astonishingly lax regime. It took some time before I accepted fully the freedom of my new surroundings. At the beginning I could not drink and smoke without suffering a Pavlovian reaction, rushing to hide the evidence, every time there was a knock on the door.

There was one other initial advantage. During the first week or so I could not work out why my fellow freshmen looked so morose. It took some time before it dawned on me that this group of eighteen year olds were understandably homesick. I was completely relaxed on that score having had my trauma at the age of eight.

I have had two golden periods in my life. The first was Cambridge and for many years afterwards nothing came close.

Some alumni remember it as an academic hothouse and fiercely demanding. It was not uncommon to hear of people having nervous breakdowns. Some were even driven to suicide. I worked very hard but felt little external pressure. When I felt intellectually sated an evening in the pub would relieve the pressure. And there was rugby, which I still enjoyed long after any delusions of real sporting achievement had evaporated. I found this a healthy outlet and a counterbalance to intellectual activity. Having considered the various societies and clubs that make up much of university life for many students, I decided not to spend time on any of them but to put most of my energies into getting a decent degree.

At the end of the first year we had preliminary exams. My results were good but not great and there was not much recognition to be had. I had worked my socks off for scant reward. At the same time, I was starting to worry about the future. What was I going to do with a second-class English degree?

I took stock and tried to be brutally honest with myself. I genuinely enjoyed literature. I had an excellent grasp of complex concepts and difficult ideas and a highly developed ability to analyse a text. I also had a superb memory and great powers of concentration. And I was a quick-witted and fluent writer. But I had little feel for poetry and was bored by detailed exegesis. And while I could soak up other people's ideas like a sponge, I had very few of my own.

In my assessment of myself, which was as objective as it could be, I was at the top of the second division but was not and never would be a top-class scholar in the mould of the best that Cambridge had to offer.

I went home and talked this through with my parents. They couldn't give me advice. They were the kindest, gentlest people but they were unworldly. They were totally without ambition or any desire for wealth or status. They wouldn't have minded if I had become the chairman of a multinational corporation, a concert pianist or a policeman as long as I was decent, honest, kind and never forgot the difference between right and wrong. They loved my sister and me equally. They were proud of us both, even though (apart from the occasional blemish) I was a star pupil, prize-winning scholar, rugby captain and leader, while my sister's life at that time was at best unsettled and frequently in turmoil. They never put me under any pressure to succeed, it all came from within, but in their quiet undemonstrative way they were proud of me and would have been happy if I never achieved anything of note in the rest of my time on earth.

However, I had discovered in Paris that there was more to life than books and rugby, and that far from being a bookish introvert I could be garrulous and sociable, although I had a strong preference for small groups and viewed the wider world with a degree of suspicion. In Paris I had mixed with French business people and young professionals well on their way to successful careers. I had been to smart parties and had met beautiful women. Paris left an indelible mark and I knew that I wanted more of it.

Going up to Cambridge had been a long-held ambition and it was a wonderful experience but, in some ways, it felt like going back to Sedbergh (except this time smoking and drinking were allowed and you had to argue with your tutor to get time to play rugby).

While I wrestled in quiet moments with the problem of what was to happen in the future, I got on with my studies and enjoying what Cambridge had to offer.

Such a short time. Three years of three terms each and eight weeks per term. This comes to 72 weeks in total but the influence of the place is permanent. And the friendships made last a lifetime; there was Peter Dix who had a distinguished career in education, his final appointment being Headmaster of Port Regis school; Geoff Hoon, already a budding politician while at Jesus, successful lawyer, future Cabinet minister and, despite what the press said at one time, a thoroughly decent fellow; Jon Manley, another First in English, a well-travelled and successful IT consultant and, briefly, my brother-in-law;

John Moore, retired management consultant, friend since we were thirteen, rugby teammate for seven years and the only friend who straddled both Sedbergh and Cambridge with me; Jimmy Mulville, my neighbour in Malcolm Street, Footlights star, TV actor and fellow hell raiser in the years during and after Cambridge, later, co-founder of Hat Trick, the TV production company, a very funny man, unspoilt by his success; and Tom Pearson, history teacher in Basingstoke for almost forty years and a man who combines strength with gentleness like no other human being that I know.

We lived together, worked together, played together and drank together. We were together when life stretched out before us. And we will still be together at the end.

In addition to this hard-drinking little group, there were others with whom I was close at the time but lost touch as our lives pulled us in different directions. For example, it was a rare but great pleasure see Rod Mengham, the most gifted English literature student of our generation, even if the short haired Yorkshire thug did somehow manage to outscore him in both entrance exam and finals. However, justice was done in the end and Rod, who is most affectionate when we do meet, is now back where he belongs, as one of the high officials of the college, curator of its art collection and a Reader in the university. He is a scholar, a poet and a fine man.

By the end of the third year, I was still studying hard in the hope of getting a good degree but simultaneously I was becoming increasingly concerned about the future. I was acutely conscious that the world outside was saturated with liberal arts graduates. One way I thought I might stay ahead of the herd was to outshine my competition. I had been well taught at Sedbergh and was now exposed to some of the world's finest scholars including Stephen Heath, the most brilliant man I have met in my life. Within forty minutes of meeting him any remaining thoughts I had harboured of a successful academic career had gone out of the window. I soon realised that he was head and shoulders above anyone else in the English faculty, with only one or two getting even close to him. I could have held my own against seventy-five per cent of them quite comfortably. But Stephen was special and he could think things that I would never have thought. He had an astonishing ability to dissect the most difficult works. He was rumoured to be translating *Finnegan's Wake* into French, and although that may not have been true, it is a measure of the awe in which he was held that people would even suggest it.

I got off to a difficult start with Stephen. At our first meeting I was subjected by him to a petulant outburst about rugby training versus English supervision that was unworthy of his towering intellect. He only respected me once he realised that, while I might have been a public school boy with a taste for blood sports, I was_serious about work. In the end, in his way, he actually rather liked me.

We developed a rapport, 'You will have to choose between rugby and me.'

'Please stop calling me Sir, we are not in the army.'

'Why do you want to waste time on a writer like Hemingway?'

'OK, if it keeps you happy we can have your supervision on your own at 10 pm this evening.'

'Your essay on D. H. Lawrence/Sophocles/Chekhov, which as usual you handed in well ahead of time, is an excellent piece of work, thoroughly researched, carefully argued, fluent and shrewd.'

'Michael, you are ready to sit your Finals with a term to spare, the only risk now is that you get stale. Take some time off, read something different like Thomas Mann's *The Magic Mountain*, go the cinema, play some rugby, just don't hurt yourself.'

'Let me tell you what Michel Foucault said about the mythology of sport. I wrote it down just for you.'

'Mike, thanks for coming round, I wanted to see you before the Finals results are published tomorrow. I have some very good news for you, you were awarded an upper First, one of the top three in the university.'

Stephen Heath had showed me the way to the summit. I believe to this day that I was so well read and well taught by my English teacher at Sedbergh that, by the time I matriculated, I could have gone through the three years at Cambridge without reading a single book or attending a single lecture and still achieved a comfortable 2:1. As it was I had my First and the Samuel Taylor Coleridge Prize, awarded to the outstanding student in an arts subject for that year. I could mark up another triumph.

So why did I work my fingers to the bone and why resist the siren calls to join my friends in the bar? Why did I push myself to the limits on a subject that I no longer had any intention of pursuing afterwards? To stay ahead of the herd? Certainly. But there was something else at play.

Surprisingly, Howard Erskine Hill provided the insight. After I graduated I wrote to thank him for three years of guidance and support and told him that I didn't know what I was going to do but I was not going to pursue an academic career. He immediately sent a cordial, thoughtful letter saying that I was easily good enough to have a successful academic career, and that even in those hard times funding for a PhD would be a formality. But then he hit the target. He wrote, 'You have read massively and to good effect. I admire the discipline and energy with which you have approached everything you have done during your time at Cambridge. I have never questioned your determination to succeed. I have sometimes questioned your motivation. Were you driven by a love of your subject or by a desire for success and for recognition? I believe you have made the right decision.' Recognition – the best medicine for rejection. It made sense to me.

Chapter 7 - After Cambridge

'Would that I were not that which I am now, nor yet become the thing I wish to be.' A. H. Clough, *Amours de Voyage*

The years after Cambridge were difficult for me and largely unrewarding.

My friends seemed to go through a tough few months of adjustment and then to embark, with more or less enthusiasm on the path that they had set for themselves. A few, like Jimmy (acting and producing), Geoff (politics), Tom and Peter (teaching) knew exactly where they were heading. Everyone I knew seemed to have some sort of plan. And some had already laid the foundations of their careers by playing prominent roles in Footlights or editing the student newspaper as a way into journalism. They often spent as much time on such activities as on their studies.

Some had chosen vocational studies such as Law, Medicine or Engineering. Some loved their subjects so much that they would happily devote the rest of their lives to them as researchers or teachers.

In any event they had mapped out a route to the future. They were getting on with life. I cannot have been alone amongst arts graduates in having no idea at all what I wanted to do. Not a clue; all I could see were things I did not want to do.

My talents, such as they were, pointed towards teaching but the spectre of the masters' common room at Sedbergh frightened me.

The Church didn't seem a good option since I was an unrepentant sinner and an atheist, and my father advised against a career in the army because promotion was so slow in peacetime.

I had seen the problem looming before I even started at Cambridge. I was very disappointed when, at the end of the first year, I applied to change to Law but the college rejected my application. Learning the law would have given me back a clear sense of purpose and clear targets to aim for: O levels and A levels, Cambridge entrance exam, Finals, Degree. These had given me something to work for and had brought out the best in me.

I might never be a brilliant figure at the Bar or the smartest lawyer in town but at least the profession existed, it wasn't just a chimaera. Law is a combination of logic and language; I was proficient in both. I was confident that with my work ethic, rational approach and excellent memory that I could have made decent fist of it. Close friends agreed and our family solicitor had suggested it years ago, even before I passed my A levels. But now I knew it was too late.

I felt that I had frittered away three valuable years reading a subject which, while interesting and enjoyable, was no use to man nor beast.

My view had been reinforced during the months before I matriculated by various family members and friends who had all had asked me the same question. 'I hear you have won a scholarship to Cambridge, that's fantastic news. Many congratulations. What are going to study there? English? English what? English literature?' (Audibly losing interest) 'And what are you going to do with that? Oh, I see, well I hope you can find the right kind of job. There is always teaching of course.'

Yes, there was always teaching and with hindsight it might well have been the best option for someone with my limited range of ability. Not all schools were like Sedbergh. Not all common rooms were as full of eccentrics, hiding from the world.

Instead of wasting a decade trying to find my place in life I could have settled comfortably into a career in teaching. In this respect, I envied Peter Dix and his beautiful wife Lizzie. With apparent ease and little self-doubt, Peter moved seamlessly, after graduating from Cambridge, to a job at King's College Choir School and on to increasingly senior positions at King's School Canterbury. Here they bought their first house in which they made a happy home. Later, they moved into a fine school house, and later still to Dorset upon Peter's appointment as headmaster of Port Regis – one of the top schools of its kind in the country. Of course, this was not achieved without a great deal of hard work and talent but Peter and Lizzie and their two beautiful daughters Becky and Emma seemed to set the gold standard for finding a balance between careers, ambition, work and family. I know of no more close and happy a family than the House of Dix. You can feel the harmony when you walk through the front door. I am proud to have Becky as my goddaughter.

So why shouldn't I follow such a shining example? After all, teaching is an important and respectable profession and many, much more intelligent people than me go into it. It is also better paid than it used to be; senior teachers command salaries comparable to those in industry. Furthermore, teaching leaves free time to pursue other interests. I started to warm to the idea; a housemaster's job at somewhere with a big reputation such as Winchester or Eton; or department head of a major grammar school or sixth form college. However, no sooner had I worked up sufficient enthusiasm for this idea to begin to do something about it than it dissolved, eaten away by the image of that masters' common room at Sedbergh on the one hand, and the memories of Paris on the other. Surely you know what you want out of life, I thought; excitement, overseas travel, money, recognition. Then all my enthusiasm would evaporate again. I kept telling myself there must be more to life than that and Paris had shown convincingly that there was.

Again, I was also influenced by friends: Nick Minns and Tom Pearson had gone into teaching and both stayed in it very happily. On the other hand John Moore graduated the year before and, armed with a respectable degree, had enrolled in a teacher-training programme in Sheffield and was already feeling restless. He would in due course get his certificate and then, following a scenic route, return to university to get an MA and evolve into a successful management consultant.

When it came to my turn to graduate I still had not decided on what I was going to do with my apparently brilliant but useless degree.

In the absence of anything better I took a job on a building site carrying concrete and general labouring throughout the long hot summer of 1976.

The company that employed me was based in Maidenhead and my girlfriend Laura had found me the job.

We had met the year before after a memorable holiday with Tom Pearson touring the Greek islands. I arrived back at Heathrow and stayed overnight in nearby Maidenhead with Jon Manley and his family, including his charming sister Laura. Laura liked me and I liked Laura. Suffice it to say that within a few months Laura was coming up to Cambridge to spend weekends with me.

For as long as I was at the university our friendship flourished, but almost as soon as the summer term of my final year ended cracks started to appear. I was feeling pretty low after the huge effort I had put into doing well in finals. Laura, too, had a problem. Her mother Peggy Manley was, to say the least, a strong-minded woman. She had three fine children and much later a fourth, Helen; but by the time Helen was born, Peggy had embarked on a career as a counsellor and was committed to it.

In the absence of a nanny, Laura was almost literally left holding the baby. Keen to get on with her own life, to spend time with me and to develop a career herself, she resented the demands made on her, and her relationship with her mother became extremely fractious. Neither would give way, and when I stayed with Laura shortly after graduation I was acutely aware of the tension.

Furthermore, her mother was coldly polite to me but I knew that she had set her heart on Laura marrying a doctor. A First from Cambridge was all well and good but not if it led to nothing better than a job on a building site. Laura, however, did not see it that way, she had set her heart on marrying me and three years after leaving university we were married in the church at Bray on Thames.

I spent the summer of 1976 considering career options but discarded them one by one, sinking deeper into depression as I did so.

I went home to talk things through with my father, who by now was fully retired after two heart attacks – the second of which almost killed him. The only advice he gave me, once we established that I had neither the interest nor aptitude in running the mill, was not to join the army or to go into teaching.

'I think you would make a fine officer,' he said, 'but the promotion prospects are poor in a peacetime army of 80,000 compared with an army at war of 320,000. And teaching? I just think you can do better than that.'

So I went back to Maidenhead and toiled away on the building site.

I was angry with my parents for not having enough money to fund some vocational training such as the law. I was angry with Laura for not recognizing that I was in crisis. I was angry with the college for not allowing me to change to a vocational degree and, above all, angry with myself for having allowed myself to be trapped in this mess.

In the end I felt so low that I went to see a doctor, a prominent GP, in Maidenhead and described to him my state of mind. I hoped that at least he would prescribe something to give me a lift for a while. He failed completely to understand what I was telling him and was patronising and dismissive. He sent me on my way with the distinct impression that I was wasting his time.

It was twenty years before I would agree to see a doctor again. I learned the hard way to rely on myself and on sheer willpower to get me through the hard times.

Back in the squalid house on the Thames where I was renting a room, I decided to take action. Knowing that I could not count on anyone but myself, I started to write unsolicited letters to organisations that I thought might be receptive to someone with my limited range of skills.

I realised that even as merely a writer, I needed to adapt my style in a way that might appeal to organisations that valued clear concise English. The dense, clotted prose beloved of many academics had contaminated me. I knew that, if I wanted to make a living from writing, I had to find a style that was simple, accessible and interesting. As a start I reread Orwell, Hemingway and the leaders in *The Times,* which was then still a fine newspaper. I made a conscious effort to rid my writing of the obscure jargon of many academics (especially the second rate) and to try to develop my own style, which was spare, taut, lapidary and allusive.

I had been led to believe (mostly at Sedbergh) that a First from Cambridge would result in any number of red carpets being laid out in my direction and so I started at what I thought was the top and sent crisp, well-written letters to a number of prominent organizations which I felt sure would fall over themselves in their haste to recruit me.

I waited for the invitations to interview and the subsequent offer letters to come flooding in.

Wrong. Without exception they all turned me down.

The BBC took me to a final interview for a coveted place on their management training scheme before telling me during the interview, in the most insulting, condescending way, that I was quite unsuited to a career in broadcasting and really ought to be kept out of harm's way and locked up in a university library. At first, I thought this was a clever interviewing technique to see how I would respond to pressure. But as time went by I realised that it was simply an interrogation by a group of unpleasant, insecure people with large but fragile egos trying to impress each other and me. I terminated the interview, saying that I agreed with them, I was quite unsuited to the BBC.

Many years later I met a charming, highly intelligent man who it turned out had been treated in exactly the same patronising way a decade earlier. A double First in History from Cambridge, he was now retired but had ended his career as editor of *The Sunday Times*. He had not forgotten how he had been treated by the BBC. Nor did I.

That was just the beginning. I had thought at one stage of becoming a journalist because of the obvious connection with writing. I was not remotely interested in provincial reporting. Covering flower shows for *The Huddersfield Examiner* did not seem the kind of apprenticeship that I had in mind. I wanted to travel and write about important things in interesting places. Given my interest in history and particularly military history, I thought I had at last cracked it. My ambition now was to become a war correspondent. All the pieces fitted together at that point and everything felt just right.

For a man with a First from Cambridge, I felt I had the right to go in at the top. I wrote a very good letter to Reuters, made up of short words and short sentences. I explained why they should recruit me while they had the chance. They replied very quickly as one would expect from such an organisation. But they turned me down flat. No explanation, no regret. My career as a dashing foreign correspondent filing first-rate dispatches from the world's hot spots was stillborn.

Next, advertising. You could make good money in advertising and my potential as a copywriter was surely not in question. I thought of applying for a job in advertising but discarded that idea almost immediately. Writing copy to convince the public of the advantages of a particular brand of baked beans or toothpaste? After three years reading

Dostoyevsky, Flaubert and Eliot... it was never going to happen.

In a state of increasing desperation, I briefly took a job with EMI but only to provide a little income while I prepared for and sat the civil service examinations. I passed, but it must be admitted, not with flying colours. The only part of the civil service that interested me was the Foreign and Commonwealth Office. They invited me for a first interview, decided I was not sufficiently diplomatic to be a diplomat and politely suggested that I look elsewhere. I think they probably had a point.

The British Council, often depicted as the poor man's FCO, granted me an interview and then asked me back for another, and another. In the end, after several hours of conversation with increasingly senior and unimpressive officers, I think they judged me politically unsound, and felt I was too right wing for their taste. They probably had a point too.

Almost at the end of my tether I wrote directly to the editor of *The Times* asking about employment opportunities there. He had the decency to write back to say that my academic credentials were impressive and that if I could write to him again in three years' time, when I had some relevant experience of (provincial) journalism under my belt. Unfortunately, and perhaps unfairly, *The Times* at that time was the only newspaper that interested me. I asked myself again; how the hell are you supposed to take an interest in regional flower shows when you have sat up all night in a Paris hotel in January reading Dostoyevsky? The thought of spending three years (or more if I couldn't break out) covering local news for *The Huddersfield Examiner*, a town that offered less significant action than a play by Samuel Beckett, was more than I could tolerate. It was almost as bad as the image of the masters' common room at Sedbergh, and it was too high an entry fee for a profession that in the main I despised anyway.

My last port of call before heading back to teacher training college was on a representative from the secret world. Like many young men before me I had been fascinated by the concept of espionage and the thought of being a spy was attractive, although I was not so naïve as to think it bore the slightest resemblance to the world of James Bond.

The first meeting I had, which was arranged through an old contact at Cambridge, took place over lunch at the Traveller's Club with a charming man who invited me to call him John. He was a deputy director of the Security Service.

The second meeting was another lunch, this time with a senior officer of the Secret Intelligence Service, also called John, at Shepherd's restaurant. He talked about the work but did it in such an elliptical way that I could barely understand what he was saying. He seemed to suggest that there was room for bright patriotic people who would do dirty and occasionally risky work for little financial reward and no recognition.

I continued this conversation at the offices of both services, at Millbank and Vauxhall respectively, and also sought the views of my uncle Colin who had worked in the Registry, the giant database now digitised and shared by both services. I also consulted a serving officer in MI5 who had been at Sedbergh and whose father had been the embassy doctor in Moscow. They were less than encouraging about their employers and the conditions of service, and seemed to regard their jobs as a kind of patriotic burden to be endured rather than enjoyed. My uncle was emphatic; if you want to make money (which I did) find something else to do.

Thus it was that after a frustrating and depressing year of letter writing, interviews, and rejection slips, I felt that I was going nowhere. I was just a penniless arts graduate with no special skills, no contacts and no prospects. All my friends seemed to be getting on with their lives. Mine was frozen. How was it, I asked myself, that in less than twelve months I had gone from being a top student in a world-class university, on fire with enthusiasm and academic achievement, to a forgotten nobody.

Many years later a neurologist who was carrying out an examination to see if I was fit for brain surgery asked if I had ever contemplated suicide. I admitted it had crossed my mind in 1977-78.

'How did you plan to kill yourself?' he asked gently.

'At first I planned to go to Zurich or Basle,' I said, 'and go to one of the euthanasia clinics. But then I had second thoughts because I want to die in my own country and not expire to the chiming of a cuckoo clock.'

He smiled.

'Also,' I continued, 'I understand that if someone buys a one-way ticket to Switzerland, the authorities in this country will investigate the circumstances very thoroughly and the surviving partner is subjected to intrusive interviews which can last for months and make him or her feel like a criminal. I didn't want to put my family through that.'

The fact was I had been thoroughly depressed since the day I left Cambridge and my retreat from life had threatened to become a rout. This state of mind continued intermittently for the next decade and, with hindsight, I should have sought professional help much earlier. Outwardly, I do not believe the signs of depression were clearly visible. Certainly, Laura never guessed or gave any indication that she did; perhaps we were both in denial. I became much quieter, taciturn, and increasingly introspective. Something had to give.

Amongst the many letters I had written to potential employers was one I had sent to the Oxford University Press in

164

response to an advertisement I had seen in *The Times Literary Supplement*. They were looking for someone to act as a kind of liaison officer between the press and British universities where many of its authors worked and many of its books were sold. I had not previously considered publishing because it was notoriously difficult to get into and badly paid. Nevertheless, OUP was an internationally known brand, universally respected and I figured that it might offer a halfway house between the academic world I had recently left, and the world to which I aspired but had not yet reached.

I duly accepted the invitation to go for an interview, not caring deeply whether I got the job or not.

I was interviewed by some senior members of the Academic Division who, unlike the brittle egomaniacs at the BBC, were pleasant, courteous and intelligent. We had a good conversation and they invited me to ask any questions. I was prepared for this and spent the next 45 minutes interrogating them on every aspect of the job and the Press. We parted on very amicable terms and sure enough a few days later a letter arrived offering me the job. The salary was meagre, as expected, but I felt I could manage and there was one perk; the job came with a company car. I wrote back immediately and accepted and was soon on my way to Oxford.

The position I was appointed to was indeed junior but my immediate boss, a delightful man called Jon Conibear, told me they had received almost 200 applications, twenty of them with PhDs.

I asked him why they had done me the honour of selecting me.

He laughed and said, 'You gave us no choice. You answered our questions and then you took control of the interview and interrogated us. By the end we were not sure if we were interviewing you for a job or if you were interviewing us.'

I spent the next three and a half years at OUP and got on well. The overwhelming majority of my colleagues were intelligent, friendly, educated and hard working. They enjoyed what they were doing and they were good at it. The OUP is a department of the University and under no obligation to make a profit although it almost always does so. Part of its remit is to fund the publishing of books that have intrinsic intellectual value but which otherwise would not be economically viable. The Press maintains a list of about 17,500 titles, far in excess of what any purely commercial house could manage. However, there were some projects that were commercially very attractive, apart from the perennial favourites such as the family of dictionaries. During my time there, the big money spinners were books in support of teaching English as a foreign language, and the darling of the press, the English Language

Teaching division, which churned out such books by the tonne for markets such as Nigeria.

I did the job I was recruited to do for about eighteen months, during which time I visited every university in the country and met a large number of academics, some of whom I liked and many of whom I did not. No experience is ever truly wasted and, apart from improving my driving skills (I was a late learner) and staying in some very pleasant hotels, particularly in Scotland (OUP was stingy on salaries but surprisingly generous with expenses), I made two important discoveries.

First, I confirmed that I had been right to abandon any idea of an academic career; it would not have suited me. I found many departments in many universities to be highly political, spiteful places where each individual had his or her own agenda, which usually involved backstabbing others, scheming for advancement or ingratiating themselves with the professor who was their head of department. Many of the lecturers, some of whom were not even very bright, possessed large but fragile egos. They would remind you of the one book they had written twenty years previously that had been the cornerstone of whatever reputation they enjoyed. They would tell you about the new book they were working on, which you knew they would never finish, or give you a copy of a paper they had presented at some obscure conference in Ostend the year before and suggest it deserved a much wider audience and the imprimatur of OUP. But much of the time they would spend sniping at the works of their colleagues ('unsound, poorly researched, highly derivative, now discredited'), and they complained endlessly about their salaries and how much better off their US counterparts were. On the last point I had some sympathy because the OUP based its pay scales on the university.

Secondly I realised that this was not the right place for me. Had I been independently wealthy, I might have stayed longer, not least because I enjoyed living in Oxford (and disliked London intensely). However I did not have a cent. I knew that I would inherit nothing and had to make my own way in the world. Although I still loved books, the business of making them and selling them I found dull. Things came to a head when junior staff went on strike about some issue (I cannot remember what exactly). I disapproved of strikes on principle and I decided to make a stand by walking through the picket line outside the main gates of the Press. I walked with deliberate slowness along the two lines of picketers. I knew that publishing staff are not the same types as miners but, while I did not expect to be beaten with pick handles, I was prepared for at least some educated abuse. However, they took no notice of me at all; they were too busy talking about their next skiing holiday. There was a distinctly upper-class air about OUP, and a quick look through the telephone directory list showed: Asquith, Conibear, Huws, Davies. This was clearly not a working men's club. I knew my time there was limited.

Shortly afterwards, I moved to a new job within the international division where I shared an office with Roger Boning, later the finance director. He was and is one of the most pleasant people I have ever met through work and we remained in touch after I left the Press. My other friend from the OUP, Alastair Scott, was away running the business in Nigeria and I never met him during my time at the Press. We became friends years later when he was running OUP's business in Hong Kong.

My new beat was the Middle East and I spent the next eighteen months travelling round the region exploring the possibilities and the challenges of publishing in that part of world. Much to Roger's consternation, I used to come back with pirated editions of some of the dictionaries and other OUP textbooks. They were reminders of the difficulties faced by publishers in developing markets, a problem that can only be tackled ultimately by governments.

I did not accomplish much at OUP and my mind was constantly distracted, visiting and revisiting over and over again the unanswered question of what I was going to do with my life. Certainly, it wasn't going to be publishing. In fact, I was sleepwalking most of my time. I made only two contributions of any note.

The first was a report, based on my travels around the UK, supporting the relaunch in paperback of most of the old World Classics series. When I had finished drafting it I sent it to the head of the paperbacks department who, for some reason, thought it brilliant and sent it to the lofty personage who rejoiced in the title of the Secretary to the Delegates or, as he would be known in any 'normal' company, the chief executive. I had been introduced to him when I joined the Press and was invited to see him again. Robin Deniston, an affable man, also waxed lyrical about the paper and said that it showed a first-class mind at work. He predicted great things for me if I stayed. I was baffled because I thought it a good but not exceptional piece of work. However, the Press acted on my recommendations and relaunched the series with minor modifications. I was pleased to learn later that it had done well. However, since the OUP has been publishing for 500 years it is likely that it would have prospered with or without my contribution.

The second and the only other concrete achievement, following what was presented to me as a modest promotion, was to lay the foundations of an Arabic translation programme of Oxford medical and scientific textbooks. This required shuttling backwards and forwards between Alexandria and

Milan and between Milan, Damascus and Baghdad. It was gratifying to learn later that the programme had gone well and that the OUP, the translator's team and the universities all benefited.

But when all was said and done, I was still living in a damp, two-bedroom flat in Walton Crescent where street prostitutes used to ply their trade at night. Meanwhile OUP's human resources department rewarded my promotion by taking away my company car and declining to increase my salary by anything like the equivalent.

It was time to move on, and by now I had abandoned any hope of ever joining one of the organisations that had comprised my original shortlist. However, I wasn't quite ready to give up all hope.

I wrote to the bluest of blue chips: Shell. And to my pleasant surprise they wrote straight back and said they would like to meet me.

I duly went to the Shell Centre, that vast building on the south bank at Waterloo. Even for someone accustomed to important meetings in tall buildings, there is something daunting about entering Shell for the first time. It may be the Stalinist architecture or it could be the shadow of the founder Henri Deterding, a friend of Adolf Hitler, but it is not immediately an encouraging place. Nevertheless, on the three occasions I went there for interviews (Shell is nothing if not thorough), and the human resources people treated me with great courtesy.

I was invited back to meet senior staff in the Shell International Public Affairs function. Here, on the thirteenth floor of the corporate headquarters of one of the world's largest and best-known multinationals, at long last I met a kindred spirit in a position of real influence.

Donald Stephenson was officially second-in-command in the department, although I was to discover later he effectively ran it. Now in his late fifties he had been *The Times* correspondent in New York and Washington. He seemed to know everything and everyone and counted Ian Fleming amongst his close friends.

I felt an immediate rapport with Donald and decided to tell him of the difficult time I had had since graduating. I unburdened myself as I had with no one else and described my intense resentment of the way life had treated me since I graduated. I had been getting on really well, I said, but now it felt like I had fallen over the edge of a cliff.

It is not a recommended way to begin a job interview.

However, Donald listened to my rant without interrupting, nodded occasionally and waited for me to finish. Then he said, 'You know, Cambridge is a wonderful university but its problem has always been that there aren't nearly enough attractive women to go round.' We both laughed.

Then turning serious, he said, 'I understand completely, Michael. The same thing happened to me. I got a First in History and a boxing blue from Cambridge, waited for the glittering prizes to arrive, and all I got was a tonne of rejection slips; although in my case, in those days, it was probably because I didn't go to the right school.'

I knew immediately that he would offer me a job and when he took me through to meet the big boss, the Coordinator, I sensed that it was just a formality. This man had a desk big enough to land a small plane on, but no papers and no discernible personality. Oddly, he showed Donald far more deference than Donald showed to him. It turned out later that Shell used to reserve this position as a pre-retirement job for burnt-out top executives or those who had failed spectacularly and whose position was essentially untenable. Few had any communication skills. For them this was an elephant's graveyard which, at least in theory, gave them and the function 'face' while the real work, and the real power, lay with Donald who was known as the real expert and who wielded very considerable influence in the entire Royal Dutch Shell group.

There was a very senior executive with an office next to the Coordinator's but no one knew what he did. We all believed that he was with MI6 (and indeed he probably was).

My meeting with the Coordinator was formal but pleasant. He asked me questions about politics and current affairs, and I did my best to answer them while Donald sat beside me saying, 'That's right, that's right,' and nodding vigorously. Afterwards, he said, 'That went well. I think you can expect to hear from us soon. If you want a career where you get your name up in lights, don't work for a giant company like Shell, work for yourself. But if you want an interesting job with a window on the world, a very international dimension and if you would like to earn more than most managing directors in Britain earn, this could be just the thing for you – and by the way I think you would be very good at it.'

When the offer arrived a fortnight later I accepted it without even bothering to read the huge 'booklet' of terms and conditions of employment that came with it.

I felt at last that I was getting on with life.

As it turned out, I spent five years at Shell. They were not particularly fulfilling years, but neither were they disappointing. At least I was back on the rails with some sense of where I was going.

Donald remained my mentor and friend until his retirement two years later. He also taught me a great deal about how international companies manage their reputations amongst those who can do the most good and most harm. And he taught me a great deal of practical tradecraft in the art of professional communications. By the time he retired he had passed on to me pretty much all he knew. Or so he said.

Sadly, they were lessons the company itself forgot several years later when it became engulfed in a scandal about the deliberate mis-stating of oil reserves. I believe that was an aberration. When I worked for Shell, albeit as a tiny cog in a giant wheel, it was a good company with excellent management, a clear set of values and a genuine sense of its social and environmental responsibilities. In short, it was a world-class brand, but it was also bureaucratic and slow to change.

The quality of people was first rate, and all the senior executives I met seemed to have a degree and MA from Oxford, Cambridge or Imperial, or three engineering degrees from Delft University in Holland. It surprised me that people of such intellect and ability should work happily in total anonymity all their lives, but apparently they did.

I had three interesting jobs in the five years I spent at Shell and in the course of my work travelled throughout Europe, South America and Africa.

By 1984 I had been promoted and was handling government relations with the UK and EU and getting on fairly well. However, I wanted to live overseas for a few years for reasons that were partly professional, partly financial and partly personal. I had rather blotted my copybook with Shell by turning down a posting to Oman. Although spending time there would not have been a problem, it would not have been my first choice and the job was totally unsuitable for me. Had Donald Stephenson not retired, the situation would never have been allowed to develop. Expatriate terms and allowances notwithstanding I was not going to sell myself short.

Then in late 1984 I received a call from a head-hunter which was to change my life entirely for the better, and launch me into my second golden age.

Shortly after I joined Shell, Laura and I were divorced. It was a marriage that should never have taken place. She had been desperately keen to get married because she was a natural wife and mother – and because she saw in it a way of escaping from her own domineering mother. On her birthday in the autumn after I left Cambridge in 1976, I had asked her what she would like; she led me to a jeweller in Windsor and pointed to some rings in the window. Her meaning was clear.

On that occasion I held firm and said it was far too soon. I needed to sort out my career first and save up some money. This produced floods of tears for several days. This upset me because I was still very fond of her and didn't want to hurt her. I was in a state of deep depression at that stage and going through the motions of living but not fully engaged.

After several months of cooling off, she raised the subject again and this time I said. 'OK let's get married.'

I regretted it almost immediately, but by this time her family had got into gear and was cranking up the whole wedding apparatus.

As the day grew closer I became more and more certain that it was a big mistake but, hating confrontation and knowing what sort of a reaction a cancellation would cause, I lacked the guts to call a halt and to my endless shame allowed it to proceed.

Finding myself on my own again was a relief rather than a sorrow. I plunged back into work with renewed vigour and was given a job that required a great deal of international travel.

When I was at home I met up with Jimmy Mulville and we continued our sybaritic ways, or 'shenanigans' as he now refers to them, sometimes in the company of the late, great comedian, Mel Smith. We misbehaved badly but without regrets.

I also made another lifelong friend. Tim Westman worked for Shell UK while I worked in Shell International. So vast was the company that we might not have met for many years, had not he been sent on one of the courses I was running at a large country house in Hertfordshire. We hit it off from the start and discovered that we both lived in Teddington. Thereafter, we met often, going for regular training runs in

Bushey Park or, almost as frequently, to the pub next door to his house. When the chance came to work abroad with HSBC, and I was hesitating because I had just received a lucrative offer to stay in London, it was Tim who urged me to take the plunge and go overseas. As it turned out it was the best piece of advice I ever had.

Chapter 8 - Hong Kong

'What you must realise about the Chinese...'

That phrase would roll around in my head so often, and it made me wince every time I heard it, and now, as I settled into my seat for the long Cathay Pacific flight to Hong Kong, I was hearing simply the latest iteration of the British expatriate mantra.

In the course of my travels I had already come to the conclusion that, essentially, there were two types of expatriate.

One was impressive, intelligent, sophisticated and included professionals such as lawyers, architects, diplomats, international bankers and spies. These people feel at home and comfortable on half a dozen different continents and sometimes speak several languages fluently. They understand both intellectually and intuitively the cultures they are working in, they are modest and respectful when dealing with local people and they make a point of saying positive things about their host's city or country. The best take on the manners of their hosts to the point where they are accepted into the community as 'one of us'. You can take this type of expatriate anywhere and be certain he won't embarrass you.

The second type was different. This species is of the 'I know my Africans' variety, and their idea of learning a foreign language is to speak English very loudly. They talk in telegramese. 'Sorry. Car broke down. Big end. Damn nuisance. Can't stop. Late already. See you at Carruthers. 8pm. Sharp.'

The defining characteristic of the second type of British expatriates, however, is the irresistible urge to recreate Guildford wherever they go. This is most easily achieved in compounds like those in Brunei, Saudi Arabia, Oman or Colombia. The men work long hours because they are being very well paid to do so. The wives want to recreate the memsahibs in Paul Scott's masterful, elegiac *Staying On*; they sit around the pool watching their children play, while drinking G and Ts. Their favourite topic is the quality of the servants. They should enjoy it while they can because twelve months from now when Jim or Wayne or Darren's contract is up, they will have saved enough to put down a deposit on that new 'executive' house they fancied in Basingstoke. They had planned to buy it outright by the time they get back with a fistful of dirhams. House prices, however, have more than doubled and, in order to pay the huge mortgage, she will have to go back to the job she had before and will once again put her shoulder to the wheel as a checkout girl in Tesco. Meanwhile their immediate concerns are the aging effect the sun is having on the skin and getting the waiter's attention. She has called out 'Boy!' loudly but the lazy sod has not taken a blind bit of notice.

'As I was saying…,' intoned my garrulous fellow passenger (clearly Type 2).

The captain announced that we were an hour away from Hong Kong and apologised again for the delay in leaving Gatwick but that we expected to land on time.

'As I was saying…,' repeated my determined neighbour.

I had dozed off for a few hours and, for all I knew, he had been telling me all night about the things I should realise about Hong Kong and the Chinese.

'What you must realise about the Chinese is they have not the slightest interest in politics.'

In June 1989 when there were a million Hong Kong people on the streets of Hong Kong, expressing their horror at what the People's Liberation Army had done to the students in Tiananmen Square I thought of calling this gentleman and asking him what he thought now of the indifference of Hong Kong people to politics. Fortunately, perhaps, I had lost the name card which he had given me when he suggested we might meet up for a drink some time with, 'It's been really good to meet you. I have enjoyed our conversation.'

Landing at the old airport was a famously dramatic experience as the plane flew along a mountainside before performing a sharp right turn and seemed to be on the point of getting snagged on the washing lines of the people who lived a few feet below.

After clearing the organised chaos of the arrival, I was pleasantly surprised to be met, greeted and warmly welcomed by my new boss.

We were driven away from the airport past some apartment blocks that, fleetingly, made my spirits drop. I had wanted to travel and to live abroad but the places I had in mind were Sydney, Rio de Janeiro or Cape Town. I did not relish the prospect of living next to a multi-storey car park for the next two years.

However, I didn't feel down for long. Once we reached the harbour I could see what a magnificent city it was. We took a car ferry, rather than the cross-harbour tunnel, so that I was able to enjoy the view of both the island and Kowloon. Stunning, I thought, absolutely stunning.

Then we drove through the Aberdeen tunnel to the south side and the calm, quiet beauty of Shouson Hill with its country club and fine houses.

By the time we reached Repulse Bay I was soaring. And there, right in the middle of the bay, we turned off the road and up a driveway with the sign Fairmount Terrace at the top. The driver and I got my things out of the car and the three of us took the lift to the seventh floor. My boss produced some keys and handed them to me with a smirk. 'Open it,' he said, 'compliments of the Bank.'

I opened the door and saw what looked like an enormous apartment, three times the size of the tiny flat I had left behind in Teddington. Then I went in and turned left and saw the view through the big windows that opened up to a balcony from the sitting room, and the view of the beach, sea and islands. I knew instinctively and with absolute certainty that this was the best decision of my life. Now I was really getting on.

My initiation was instructive. I had agreed with my new employers that I would start my contract on a certain date, a Monday. I had booked a flight which would mean arriving the previous Friday morning. Not having been to Hong Kong before, I wanted to take some time to familiarise myself and planned to take a shower before going out to explore my new surroundings.

However, in a move that at the time seemed slightly odd (I would discover more) and a sign or statement of authority, my new boss started looking at his watch and urged me to change into a suit.

We then drove straight to the Bank's temporary headquarters and I was taken to meet a very important person who enjoyed the title of Group Staff Controller. An affable man, he gave me a warm welcome. He said, 'We were not expecting you until Monday but it's good to have you on board.' He proceeded to change the date on my contract to the day I arrived.

Thus it was that two hours after arriving in Hong Kong I was enrolled as an officer of The Hongkong and Shanghai Banking Corporation and given an office with a desk, a chair and a telephone and told to get on with it. Get on with what?

In a way, I was a complete beginner. I had never been to Hong Kong. I had done a little background reading on the territory and on the Bank ahead of my interviews.

In the past my preparation for interviews was thorough, and my approach to them serious. But on this occasion it was cavalier, because I wasn't sure I wanted to go there and was being headhunted at the time by another big company.

'How much do you know about banking?' they had asked.

I had replied, 'Well, I have an overdraft.'

They must have found this vaguely amusing or I would not have found myself sitting in a high-rise building, looking at the harbour.

It was soon apparent that in this part of the world the Bank was massive. In fact, the Bank dominated the commercial life of the local economy to an extent not seen anywhere else in the world, except perhaps the car companies in Detroit in their heyday. The cliché was that the top jobs in Hong Kong were the Governor, the President of the Jockey Club and the Chairman of the Bank, but not necessarily in that order. It was also said that the Chairman of the Bank was quite happy with the Jockey Club and did not want the other job.

The Bank performed some of the functions that in many countries are carried out by the central banks. The most visible was the issuing of banknotes. It operated the clearing system on behalf of the Hong Kong Association of Banks, which it chaired and which set interest rates on certain retail deposits. From time to time, although not a lender of last resort, it stepped in to support smaller banks. These included the Hang Seng Bank, the territory's second largest bank, which had suffered a liquidity crisis in 1962 but which otherwise was an excellent bank and in which Hongkong Bank maintained a majority shareholding. The Hongkong Bank was frequently accused of enjoying special privileges – an accusation that it denied strenuously.

In summary, the Bank was by some distance the biggest show in town. Its shares were widely held and many Hong Kong people, the most financially literate in the world, followed its fortunes closely. It was often said that what was good for Hong Kong was good for Hongkong Bank and vice versa – hence the Bank's investments in hotels, shipping and newspapers. If Hong Kong needed it, Hongkong Bank was there to finance it, provided, of course, it proved that it could make an acceptable return.

Above all the Bank enjoyed one key advantage – public confidence. In a community largely composed of refugees from Mainland China who knew what it was to lose everything, and in a city always febrile and prone to rumour and to panic, the Bank stood firm. Other banks might offer better rates or service. The Shanghainese might favour one bank, the Chiu Chow another; they would certainly never trust each other. But Hongkong Bank, The Bank, stood alone. Alone and impartial, it was a local bank but run by foreigners and therefore above the fray.

In 1985 joining the Bank was like joining a family, albeit one soon to be led by a Victorian patriarch. It was a paternalistic organisation which recruited for the long term and which rewarded competence, loyalty, integrity and hard work. It looked after its own and it was strong on individual accountability. If you made a mistake and owned up to it, people rallied round to help you sort out whatever had gone wrong. Making the same mistake twice was considered unhelpful. Being found out covering up a mistake was terminal.

My first chairman was Michael Sandberg, later knighted and ennobled. Physically small but relentlessly energetic, he had led the Bank for a decade by the time I joined it, embarking on a strategy of internationalisation while strengthening its position at home.

I wrote some speeches for him and he seemed to quite like them. I was able to capture his impish sense of humour. He was certainly courteous and pleasant to deal with but he retired in 1986 and so I never really got to know him.

His successor, Willie Purves, was by any standards a remarkable man. From an ordinary background in lowland Scotland he first came to note when winning the DSO in the Korean War, the youngest national serviceman ever to do so.

The more you got to know Willie, the more you liked him, but on first meeting he was daunting. Large, though not quite as big as at first appeared, powerfully built with a military bearing, he had enormous charisma and when he entered a room full of people you could see several dozen pairs of eyes swivel towards him. Possessed of an extremely loud voice, he appeared to be in a state of perpetual rage against the follies of mankind. He was daunting until you spotted the twinkle in his eye.

When, in 1992, I was promoted to the hot seat and reported directly to him, each day began with a bruising ritual. At exactly 08.02 the telephone would go and I would try to pick it up before the second ring, knowing who was calling without needing to look at my screen to see the number 1122 appear.

'Purves,' he would snarl, and then launch into a rant, complaining about something he had seen or read or heard overnight.

He was particularly angry with the business editor of the *South China Morning Post,* although he often wrote about Willie admiringly. 'Why does that bloody man, John Mulcahy always call me forceful and aggressive?' he would roar. 'I'll show that bastard what it means to be aggressive.' And then he would rage against whatever else was on his mind, ranging far and wide. It might be the collapse of the Soviet Union or a rogue ATM in Manila. You were left with the distinct feeling that it was all your fault and that you should do something about it immediately.

At the end of his daily monologue he would yell 'Coral!' and Coral Craik, his marvellous and imperturbable Scottish secretary, would enter the room.

Before he hung up without another word you might hear her say, 'You bellowed, Chairman?'

Willie Purves possessed an incredible capacity for work, limitless energy, an elephantine memory, a volcanic temper and a heart of gold. To this day, he is the only man I have ever known who could wish you Merry Christmas and make it sound like a threat.

He would ask you a question, then answer it and then tell you were wrong before you even had time to open your mouth.

It was said that when you worked for him you needed to know nine words, 'Yes, no, I don't know, but I'll find out.' I tried to make do with fewer.

Max Hastings, former editor of the *Daily Telegraph*, described a lunch with him as like 'a meeting with an Old Testament prophet'.

By the time Willie became chairman there had been some changes in our department. The contract of the head of it was not renewed. His successor was George Cardona, a First in PPE from Oxford who had been a special adviser to Margaret Thatcher and, at one stage, the Finance Minister of Vanuatu.

George and I were both considered for the same job but he had more relevant experience and was better qualified. However, the Bank decided that they liked the cut of my jib. They also felt that what lay ahead would bring more than enough work for us.

George was an extremely able man, articulate, persuasive, quick witted, always ready with a solution to every problem, hardworking and ambitious. In most respects he was brilliant, probably the best head of public affairs the Bank ever had. I was appointed his deputy and I think it fair to say I was a more gifted writer. As a team we established an influential unit within the Bank just at the point when it most mattered.

There were already some very capable and talented people in the department when we joined it, but the Bank had shackled them while it came to terms with what was required.

The recent past was already instructive. A few years before, in 1981–82, it had bid unsuccessfully for the Royal Bank of Scotland but had been rebuffed by the Edinburgh establishment and by the opposition of the Governor of the Bank of England. It was essentially a government relations and communications issue.

When I first arrived in Hong Kong, the Bank was still cleaning up another public relations disaster. Public concern focussed on the construction of the Bank's futuristic new headquarters building, which was rumoured to have cost so much that it threatened the financial stability of the institution.

The truth was that there had been significant cost overruns on certain parts of construction, but the Bank made a bad situation worse with its obsessive secrecy.

The situation was serious because it threatened to undermine public confidence and thereby threaten the Bank's unique position in Hong Kong. In the early weeks I felt that I had joined a property company not a bank, so preoccupied was everyone with the problem.

Eventually, the Bank listened to its own communications experts and under the leadership of a long serving and highly capable member of the department, Nanette McClintock, the very negative stories were turned round.

Within a year, the Bank's senior management and its architect, Sir Norman Foster, were patting each other on the back as the reviews became ever more positive.

Soon after, we were offering guided tours around what was widely lauded as a masterpiece of modern architecture. In the enthusiasm, the fact that it had cost too much was eventually forgotten.

When all was said and done, the fuss over the building was an unwelcome distraction. The real objective was to manage the Bank through an issue which no other bank in the world had faced, the impending transfer of sovereignty. Under the terms of the Joint Declaration and the ensuing Basic Law, Hong Kong was given specific and detailed guarantees that its highly distinctive lifestyle, i.e. unfettered capitalism, and its economic and personal freedom would be preserved for at least fifty years.

The problem was that no one knew how it would work out in practice, and since most Hong Kong people were refugees or the sons and daughters of refugees, many had their suspicions. Their confidence was not improved by the bloody suppression of student demonstrations in Tiananmen Square in

June 1989, and by the row between the last Governor, Chris Patten, and Beijing over the pace of democratic reform.

Our task, in essence, was to help steer the Bank through the choppy seas ahead and hopefully land it safely on the other side, with its reputation intact with its various publics: Hong Kong (everyone); London (the financial community); and Beijing (the government). The chances of getting it absolutely right were small and the chance of someone causing an accident through an ill-timed comment or action was very high. The situation required considerable skill and pushed my department right into the front line, conferring an influence on it that otherwise it would probably not have enjoyed.

There was a graphic example of how badly communications could go wrong when mismanaged. In the immediate aftermath of the promulgation of the Joint Declaration, Jardine Matheson, openly admitting concerns about 1997, had announced that it was moving its head office to Bermuda. This severely damaged the fragile public confidence in Hong Kong, triggering a collapse in the stock market, a collapse in Jardine's own share price and a wave of criticism locally and from Beijing. The Princely Hong of James Clavell fame has never fully recovered. Once enjoying the same market capitalisation as the Bank, it is now 14 per cent of HSBC (as the Bank was known around the world).

The Bank's handling of the 1997 question was altogether more sophisticated.

First, we prepared the market to expect that we were looking to make an acquisition in Europe, and we pointed out that this had been our intention long before the future of Hong Kong ever reached the public agenda.

Then we sought and obtained approval for a Scheme of Arrangement to revise and amend the Bank's Ordinance and Articles of Association (effectively its constitution). This was presented as routine housekeeping to bring the Bank's governance up to date and because a holding company structure made acquisitions administratively easier. We did admit that there was an element of 1997 in the reorganisation, but attributed that to other banks turning us down in the markets because they did not see 1997 as we saw it.

However, while the Bank made it clear that The Hongkong and Shanghai Banking Corporation itself would remain headquartered in Hong Kong, the rewriting of our charter provided for a holding company that was based in London. Thereafter, when we acquired Midland Bank in 1992, we were able to say correctly and honestly that we were relocating the group head office to London at the invitation of our lead regulator. The acquisition of Midland, which at the time was the largest international bank acquisition in history, attracted enormous media and investor interest in London and Hong Kong, but it was mostly positive.

The UK was ready for change and for improvement in its banking and believed that HSBC was a breath of fresh air.

In Hong Kong the regular studies we commissioned to track public opinion did show some negative reaction to the move overseas of Wayfoong (the Bank's Cantonese name), but far less than the response to Jardine Matheson's bombshell eight years earlier.

Using a range of communications, we were able to reassure the Hong Kong customer base that it would be business as usual after 1997.

Later research showed that we passed through 1997 in remarkably good shape and without unsettling Hong Kong. We remained assiduously apolitical, which took a considerable effort given the many unofficial spokesmen who worked for the Bank.

As to China, we kept the government in Beijing informed all the way along. On visits to Beijing, Willie Purves and John Bond took great care to explain to senior figures in the Chinese government what we were doing and why.

The year 1992, when we acquired Midland, was a transforming year for the Bank and for me personally. Five years earlier, in December 1987, I had won my spurs by flying to London overnight and in total secrecy. I was carrying with me a copy of the announcement that we were taking a 14.9 per cent stake in Midland. My briefcase never left my side. The reason for secrecy, on this occasion entirely legitimate, was dictated by the need to comply with stringent stock exchange requirements and to ensure that no other bank made a pre-emptive strike. By the time I reached the Bishopsgate office at about 6.30 am there was no sign of a leak and we made the announcement exactly as planned at 8 am London time.

It was a huge story in Hong Kong and Willie Purves hosted a packed press conference.

I meanwhile anchored the London end, and during the next twelve hours of intense activity I must have talked to about eighty journalists. Many of them simply wanted basic information, a reminder that while we might be a household name in Hong Kong, we were barely known in the UK. Some journalists were looking for an angle (as journalists do) and inevitably it was 'Bank escapes before the Communists arrive,' but I felt that I had talked most of them down.

Eventually, I left the office at about 9 pm and walked back to my hotel (booked after the announcement). I had some dinner but was still wide awake, so having showered and rested for a couple of hours, early the next day (the third without sleep), I walked back into the city and bought first editions of all the national newspapers.

Our announcement was not only the biggest business story; it was the lead story in every newspaper and the tone and overall coverage was very positive.

I faxed all the articles, eighty or so, to Hong Kong. I then called George Cardona who seemed delighted with the way things had gone and said that even Willie was pleased with the coverage.

I spent the weekend with friends in a state of elation, then returned to the office on Monday and talked to a few more journalists. These included a man from the *New China News Agency,* who interrogated me at length about the Bank's views on 1997. The NCNA is, of course, much more than a news agency.

Later that day, I flew back to Hong Kong and although I was not exactly accorded a hero's welcome, I did notice a marked warming in the way the Bank's top management treated me. The Bank was nothing if not hierarchical, and there was a distinct change to the habitually polite but rather aloof manner favoured by many senior executives in their dealings with younger international officers. John Gray, the group finance director, and David Jaques, executive director banking – two elevated personages seldom even seen by the rank and file – greeted me as a long-lost brother. Even Willie snarled his

196

appreciation the next time he saw me. Although it remained unspoken, it was clear that after serving a long apprenticeship as a competent but still untested outsider, I was now part of the family, trusted completely and entitled to know everything. I had gone from respected mercenary to brother-in-arms. I belonged. It felt good.

It so happened that the acquisition of Midland took longer to complete than originally envisaged. By 1990 it was clear that they were battling strong economic headwinds, while at the same time we were dealing with problems in some of our outlying businesses.

But by 1992 we were ready to consummate the deal. This was widely expected and so it lacked the element of excitement that the 1987 announcement had caused.

Nevertheless, it involved several months of very hard work and strenuous efforts to persuade the Midland shareholders that the deal was in their best interests. By now Hongkong Bank (arguably nudged in the right direction by G Cardona and M Broadbent) had discovered the power of *glasnost* and we went on a major offensive to establish the Bank's credentials. We flew groups of analysts, institutional shareholders and journalists around the world, from London to Dubai to Hong Kong, to Vancouver and Buffalo, to show them the global reach of our operations. They returned home jet-lagged but persuaded that we were a going concern and, crucially, that Hong Kong had a future notwithstanding the negative media coverage.

Willie Purves signed 650 letters to British MPs to argue the case for buying Midland and received wide cross-party support.

However, one snag remained; the market was signalling that our offer needed a little sweetening if we were to carry the day. At about the same time, Lloyds Bank started to mutter about the possibility of making a counter bid. Accordingly, new documents were drawn up with the advice of our investment bank and we began to think about how best to announce the offer.

It was in this connection that I found myself late one evening in Willie Purves' office discussing the announcement with David Shaw, and Kevin Westley of our investment bank. Willie had said to me, 'Of course Michael, we shall have to hold a full press conference in Hong Kong but we must plan it in total secrecy.'

'Yes, in total secrecy,' echoed David Shaw, the brilliant corporate lawyer who had worked night and day for months to construct the Scheme of Arrangement and was the legal genius behind the offer for Midland.

'I have it all in hand, Chairman,' I said chirpily. 'The level 41 conference room has been booked already.'

David Shaw went ashen and said, 'Bloody hell. That means the whole of Hong Kong knows already that we are having a press conference.'

Willie looked as though he was about to go incandescent.

Kevin Westley looked out of the window having seen something in the harbour that demanded his attention.

'I doubt it, David,' I said smugly. 'Nanette McClintock made the booking in the name of the Hong Kong Association for the Mentally Handicapped.'

Willie guffawed, David Shaw beamed and Kevin Westley clapped me on the shoulder. Thank you, Nanette, thank you Donald Stephenson.

We completed the acquisition of Midland in the summer of 1992. It effectively doubled the size of the HSBC Group but it gave me a dilemma. At the invitation of the Bank of England the Group Head Office was to relocate from Hong Kong to London, where we could more easily be invited for a cup of tea and a raised eyebrow. This relocation included the functional heads and I would be among them. However, for a mixture of personal and professional reasons I wanted to stay in Hong Kong. For one thing I wanted to see through 1997. Having lived with it for ten years already, I was reluctant to bow out at the most critical stage.

I talked it through with Willie who said, 'I want you here and I want you there. Unlike you, I don't have a choice. I have to move to London'

I chose to stay and never regretted it. The price I paid, on paper at least, was that I stepped aside and another person was given the top job in London.

Five years later, at noon on 30 June 1997, Willie Purves walked into my office and shut the door. 'Will you come and work with John and me in London?' he said.

Because he asked nicely and had already given me an extra five years in Hong Kong and was the Group Chairman, I said yes.

My last few years in Hong Kong, from the time the Group Head Office moved to London until I finally surrendered and relocated to London myself early in 1998, were, in terms of the job, some of the most enjoyable I ever had. Although it was mildly disappointing to have to give way to a new head of public affairs, I was given a great deal of independence to run Asia Pacific which, including Hong Kong, continued to account for the lion's share of profits.

For most of the time I had a charming and highly intelligent local chairman to work for in John Gray, and I had an excellent and highly motivated department. Early on, it was threatened with being drastically reduced as the new head office took shape in London. I was asked, not unreasonably, to justify why we still needed sixty people in what was now, with 1997 negotiated successfully, merely a subsidiary. However, I made a strong case, analysing the department and arguing that it was effectively five departments rolled into one and that it was giving the Group excellent value for money. The head of Group Human Resources in London, who was responsible for migrating work and jobs in one direction or another, congratulated me on paper and said that if the department had been a listed company, he would have bought shares in it. The solitary internal threat was seen off, leaving us free to do some good work and to enjoy doing it. We worked hard and we had fun.

When I left Hong Kong, which I did with great reluctance, my staff gave me a framed cartoon. It contained an element of gentle satire, prompted by what they saw as my military style of management and was drawn by the head cartoonist at the *South China Morning Post*. It included a list of 'battle honours', the crises that we had handled in my thirteen years in Hong Kong. These included: the fallout from Black Monday (the stock market crash in 1987); a major fraud committed against the Bank in Indonesia and subsequent briefings to the *Asian Wall Street Journal* against the perpetrators in order to expose them; a branch bombing in the

New Territories in Hong Kong that left eleven colleagues dead; the aftermath of Tiananmen Square killings in June 1989, which caused huge interest from around the world in the prospects for Hong Kong; a campaign to secure British passports for key Hong Kong people; the collapse of BCCI which triggered bank runs in Hong Kong; handling the impact of an illegal strike by Bank staff in Manila, which included assassination threats and the evacuation of senior executives by helicopter; the acquisition of Midland; and of course 1997. In fact, there was never a dull moment.

Sometimes, it seemed that all we did was work but that wasn't true. We were young and energetic. We worked hard and we played hard.

For a time, I enjoyed the freewheeling lifestyle of a single man in Hong Kong and carried on much as I had with Jimmy in London. Sometimes – no, often – we burned the candle at both ends. I did not expect to make any lasting friendships; Hong Kong seemed too transient, with people posted there and then somewhere else, and for a time that suited me well. But in due course I grew weary of Sunday afternoons wasted with the worst type of expatriates, trapped for hours in vacuous conversations on junk trips. I looked for more.

I was able to build some more meaningful friendships and to establish what Ernest Hemingway called the small society. The best of the friendships I made in Hong Kong survived my eventual departure and have proved lasting. They rank with those made at Sedbergh and Cambridge.

My first friend was Anthony Rademeyer, one of my earliest contacts in the Bank. We hit it off straight away despite huge language problems. When I first met him, he was working for a rising star called Stephen Green, who was a senior hire brought in from McKinsey to oversee the development of the treasury function. This had been identified as an area of growing importance to an international bank. The days when banks simply took deposits on which they paid a small amount of interest and then lent them to people at a higher rate were coming to an end. Foreign exchange, which was something that you arranged with Thomas Cook when you went on holiday to Benidorm, had apparently become a science. Banks now traded it and many other things called swaps and options, and derivatives with other banks and there were huge profits to be made if you got it right. Stephen, unusual amongst the Bank's top management at that time because he was a graduate (a First from Oxford), had assembled around him a small group of the brightest and best. Having chatted with me courteously and unpatronisingly for twenty minutes, he introduced me to Anthony with a warning that he talked and wrote with a lot of jargon. He was right. Anthony spoke a language I never really understood but he must have known what he was talking about because he had a meteoric rise though the Bank.

He could be seen in the corner office of bigger and bigger dealing rooms in London and New York, then London again, then back to Hong Kong before heading into premature but prosperous exile. He was as close as I have come to knowing a Master of the Universe, a title he always refused. He remained utterly unspoilt by his success, loyal to his roots in Zimbabwe and to his many friends around the world. Together with his charming wife Fabienne and their three delightful and talented children, they make up another of the happy, harmonious families that seem to be a feature of my friends.

Anthony and I used to work out at a gym called Raffles and it was there that I was introduced to Peter and Rohini Kedward. Ro was Sri Lankan but had grown up in Singapore. Peter was a long-term Hong Kong resident who had left England after a family tragedy and had joined the Hong Kong police. He had graduated to the Special Duties Unit (which dealt with counter terrorism, hostage rescue and other extreme situations) and been trained by Britain's SAS. Peter finished his career as Head of Security for Cathay Pacific Airways. Peter and Ro retired to Fishguard in Wales where, well into his sixties, he remains the all-action hero.

In the last couple of years in Hong Kong I made another great friend in Simon Penney. He was appointed chief financial officer of the Bank in Hong Kong during my last two years there. He was one of several Midland staff cross-posted from London as part of a talent swap to bind the enlarged company more tightly together. It would be an understatement to say that Simon took to Hong Kong and to Asia like a duck to water. His intellectual ability, which was considerable, was equalled only by his enjoyment of everything Asia had to offer. It was no surprise when, after a spell as chief financial officer of our North American operations, he chose to retire to Phuket in Thailand.

Through Anthony and Fabienne Rademeyer I also met David Beaves and very rapidly we became inseparable friends. David was in many ways the man I had wanted to be. A brilliant Cambridge-educated shipping lawyer from an ordinary background that he made no attempt to hide, he had been in Hong Kong for many years. He enjoyed all the trappings of success such as the beautifully furnished apartment on the Peak, the car with fancy headlights, the suits made by one of the territory's finest tailors and membership of the Hong Kong Club. David was (and is) an unashamed hedonist who enjoyed the best of everything. But, unlike some of his peers, he was no materialistic cipher. Beneath the banter and witty repartee was a very sensitive man who listened and understood and felt deeply. Like me, he was a man who had been through the wringer in his personal life and had taken the scenic route to matrimonial bliss. I felt extraordinarily happy for him and proud of myself when he asked me to be his best man at his wedding in Manila. It was a very grand occasion and in his bride Carmen Fernandez he found his perfect partner.

Life in Hong Kong was very pleasant – providing you had enough money.

Some people came out from the UK with nothing and tried to find a job and make their way. I had nothing but admiration for them because I believed it took courage to land in a Chinese city with 6.5 million (now incredibly 8 million) of the world's most competitive, hardworking and shrewd people. The incomers were sometimes referred to as FILTH (Failed in London Try Hong Kong), but that was an unfair label and some of them were talented people who did very well and made their fortune.

By contrast, anyone joining the Bank on expatriate terms led an extraordinarily cossetted life. They were given flats owned or paid for by the Bank that by local standards were immense. All they had to do on arrival in Hong Kong was go to their address and open the door. Even the fridges had been stocked in advance. They were expected to work hard for the privileged lifestyle they had been granted.

As my standing in the Bank drifted in the right direction, I moved from Fairmount Terrace to a bigger flat with an even better view. Thence I moved to a still more luxurious development and finally to a house on the Peak. This was considered the ultimate achievement although personally I did not much like the house and would have been quite happy to stay in Repulse Bay. Naturally, it would have been considered bad form to say so.

Property became an all-consuming obsession in Hong Kong. There was a groundswell of resentment amongst the local staff at the lavish treatment of the expatriates. However, for reasons I never understood, the Bank would not lend to its international staff to buy property in Hong Kong. And so, as the property prices began to soar in the early 1990s (and continued with pauses until they reached today's staggering levels) the expatriates could only stand and stare as their colleagues' tiny shoeboxes turned them into multi-millionaires. The grumbles of the local staff became noticeably quieter and I could see a certain justice in this.

Two other personal matters from this period are worth noting.

On leave in London in 1987 I happened to stay with Jimmy Mulville who introduced me to a friend of his who he said had been adopted. This friend (who I shall not name out of respect for his privacy) told me about a remarkable woman called Ariel Bruce. Ariel specialised in helping adopted children trace their parents. Although I had given little thought to the matter since moving to Hong Kong my interest was piqued. I went to see Ariel myself. I told her all that I knew about my natural parents, which was little enough and, having paid her modest fee, promptly forgot the matter.

I was on a business trip to Geneva a few months later when Ariel called my hotel room. 'I have found your mother,' she said, 'she is alive and well. I am sorry to say that your father died more than twenty years ago. But you should know that he was a decorated war hero and I have found some proof of that.'

The next time I was in London I went to see Ariel again. She gave me her impressions of Catherine and some copies of documents she had unearthed and suggested that I write to Catherine on my return to Hong Kong. Which I did.

We wrote to each other and exchanged photos for a few months and agreed to meet on my next leave. And this is how we came to that first, initially very difficult, meeting in Sutton in 1988.

The other thing that happened to me in Hong Kong – and by far the more important – was that I met the love of my life.

Joyce and I met through work (what else?) when she came to present some market research findings. I thought she was extraordinarily beautiful, and smart and – unusually for very attractive women – she was nice. I had no hesitation at all in flouting the usual protocols governing business relationships and asked her out. To my great surprise she accepted and so began the best and most important friendship of my life.

We took things quite slowly at first because we had both experienced previous disasters. Furthermore, after several short and unsatisfactory liaisons and having no interest in children, I did not consider myself husband material. I had more or less decided to remain single.

As our friendship developed, she stepped back from handling the Bank's business, although for the sake of absolute clarity I obtained John Gray's permission to retain her company's services. They were after all the best.

In the autumn of 1986, Joyce took me to meet her parents. I knew that they did not disapprove of me on racial grounds, because three of her sisters had married Caucasians and they had called their eldest son Winston. Clearly, however, it was an important occasion and the source of some anxiety.

It got off to a difficult start because, as we sat down to enjoy the magnificent lunch which Joyce's mother had prepared, the dining chair I sat on, unsuited to fifteen stone Gweilos, broke. In fact it didn't just break, it disintegrated into matchwood. If there had been an open fire I would have gathered up the pieces and thrown them and myself onto it. It is difficult enough to make a favourable impression when you are upright and attempting to converse in languages none of you understands. How much harder is it when you are lying on your back surrounded by the remnants of a valued piece of your hosts' furniture?

Fortunately, Joyce's parents were sweet and forgiving (traits which she inherited) and somehow I secured their approval.

With a little gentle encouragement from her father after we had lived together for four years, we were married in Moffat in Scotland on 14 June 1990.

The choice of country was dictated by Willie Purves, inevitably. He pointed out that it took less time to get married in Scotland than in England and that I therefore needed to take less leave. He was nothing if not thoughtful.

Joyce and I both had demanding jobs, and she had little interest in becoming a traditional bank wife. Indeed, she readily admits that she did little or nothing to support or advance my career.

We were both determined to have a life outside work and there was at least some time for pleasure. If you were high-minded and wanted Kultur then Hong Kong did not begin to compare with London or New York. There was an Annual Arts Festival that brought first-class orchestras, soloists, ballets and other musicians and performers to Hong Kong. But in truth it was a case of feast or famine; you were as likely to spend your Saturday evening listening to a lecture by a Nobel Prize winning economist as you were to a famous cellist. In the event much of our spare time was spent in the cinema or eating and drinking, and in shopping. And of course there was horse racing, a 'national' obsession on which the Chinese population wagered staggering sums of money. For the expatriate population (and a growing number of Chinese fans) there was the annual sporting/bacchanalia of the Rugby Sevens, an event that I had the privilege to help organise for ten years. Then of course there was the socialising – a hundred cocktail parties to celebrate a company listing on the stock exchange, a new product launch or a move to a new building.

Had it not been for Joyce, I do not think I would have had many Chinese friends or done much socialising with them. Most expatriates stayed within their own circles and so did many Chinese. One reason was language. I do not think you can really understand a society if you cannot speak the language, not necessarily fluently, but well enough to grasp the essentials. At work all our communications were in English and most colleagues spoke and wrote it fairly well. But Chinese, and more particularly Cantonese, remained a background noise, utterly inaccessible and incomprehensible. To borrow a phrase from Conrad, 'It was one of those impossible languages which sometimes we hear in our dreams'.

My own efforts to learn Cantonese did not get off the ground and I never met any non-Chinese who claimed to speak it fluently. However, with Joyce acting as my interpreter (her standard of English, drilled into her by an exemplary education at the Diocesan Girls School, puts me to shame), I believe I reached a better understanding of Hong Kong and its people than might otherwise have been the case.

The main conclusion I reached after I had spent some time in Hong Kong was that I had to unlearn much of what was considered conventional wisdom by Type 2 expatriates 'I know my Africans,' 'What you must understand about the Chinese...'

It was said that Hong Kong people were not interested in politics. Wrong.

It was said that they were only interested in making money. Wrong. They do have a healthy respect for money and work extremely hard to acquire it. But the other side of the equation is that they are extraordinarily generous to family, friends and to the wider world. Just look at the response from Hong Kong every time there is a disaster somewhere in the world. In response to an earthquake in Haiti, a famine in Ethiopia, a tsunami in Asia, Hong Kong is one of the most generous places in the world.

Two people who understood this and who became my friends in Hong Kong and even closer friends since are Nanette McClintock and Chris Bale.

Nanette was a deeply respected colleague who oversaw the charitable activities of the Hongkong Bank Foundation, and in her spare time (of which she had none) did invaluable work for the Red Cross. Nanette stayed in Hong Kong after she retired from the Bank and not even the prospect of a cottage in the south west of Ireland could persuade her to leave.

Chris, a former journalist at the *Hong Kong Standard* and an ATV newsreader, left Hong Kong after more than twenty years, having put the fear of God into the Bank's senior executives as a media trainer. Formerly a director of Oxfam in Hong Kong, he returned home, having been head-hunted to lead Befrienders International, and was honoured by the Queen.

Both Nanette and Chris were long time Hong Kong residents who were close to the community. I looked to Joyce and to them when I wanted to understand public opinion and found it a great deal more rewarding than listening to some pompous Jardine executive standing in the Captain's Bar of the Mandarin Oriental and pontificating, 'What you must realise about the Chinese is that they are not like us.'

Thank goodness for that. Vive la différence.

Chapter 9 - London

It was often said that if you stayed in Hong Kong for more than six years you could never leave. When I came back to the UK almost thirteen years after leaving, I thought that must be true. The first twelve months were difficult. I felt alien. Everything was the same and everything was different. People no longer had wives or husbands, girlfriends or boyfriends; they had 'partners'. I felt this made everyone sound like estate agents.

The pace of London, frenetic by English standards, seemed dozy by comparison with Hong Kong.

Although I had been reappointed to the top job in the Bank's communications department and given the impressive title of Director of Group Corporate Affairs and promoted, I calculated that I was 50 per cent worse off financially when re-entering the UK tax system and losing housing and other benefits. My accountant, ever helpful, said it was 55 per cent.

I recall a lunch with Chris Bale shortly after my return. Ever sensitive to other people's feelings and suspecting that I might be finding it hard going, he asked me how I was feeling.

I missed everything about Hong Kong. I said I had no idea why I had ever agreed to it. I was almost inconsolable.

HSBC in London no longer felt like a family. It felt like what it was; the meeting of two huge institutions with different characters, different values. The former Midland Bank staff all referred to 'the merger'; no-one seemed prepared to accept that Midland no longer existed as a separate, listed company. It had been acquired, taken over, bought lock, stock and barrel. It was now a wholly owned subsidiary. Inevitably, there were office politics with people jockeying for position in the enclaves of former Midland staff who could not accept the new reality. The Group Finance Director, later Group Chairman, Douglas Flint said, 'Welcome to the fiery furnace,' and, always an ally, suggested that I watch my back.

My immediate task was to combine four communications units. This in itself was a major political undertaking, because it deprived certain senior executives of their own communications apparatus and thereby reduced their autonomy. I identified a good deal of dead wood in the combined communications function, which over time would have to be disposed of, but I was asked not to make cuts immediately. However, there were some hidden treasures amongst the detritus.

My first PA, Alyson Browell, was outstanding.

When Alyson left to return home to Newcastle, her successor Elaine Martin was equally loyal, efficient and supportive.

And in the Group Archives I found an absolute gem of a team. Totally self-sufficient, it was in need of virtually no management, quietly and efficiently going about its business headed by Edwin Green, a doyen of his profession, and a fine gentleman too. We were to use HSBC's remarkable past as a powerful communications tool, in due course producing the highly respected 'HSBC History Wall' as a feature of our new headquarters.

These were the exceptions, however. Of the sixty people for whom I was directly responsible, only twenty per cent were of a standard I found acceptable and competent. And several were openly resentful that an interloper from Hong Kong had come to take over.

The view of the top, however, was very different. In Hong Kong my last line manager and I did not get on at all well and it made leaving Hong Kong that much easier. In John Bond (Willie's successor as Group Chairman in 1998), to whom I reported in London, I found the complete opposite. Demanding and decisive but willing to listen, unfailingly courteous, thoughtful, and appreciative of work well done, he was a man of absolute integrity and inspiring to work for. John had devoted his life to the Bank and was the embodiment of all its values. He was quite simply the best boss I ever had, and when he was joined by Stephen Green, as Group Chief Executive, it was my dream team.

Beyond work, it was good to be with Joyce again. She had preceded me and moved to London the year before to begin her training as a psychotherapist. And once we recovered our two dogs and cats from quarantine (which they survived, though it left its mark) we felt like a family again.

Over a year or so, I grew to like London a little bit more, to miss Hong Kong a little bit less and to enjoy what Europe had to offer. In many ways it was more attractive than much of Asia. After taking short holidays to France and Spain, I started to explore and consider the possibility of living in continental Europe when we retired. Joyce did not share my enthusiasm and so we settled in England instead.

Not having lived in London before, Joyce did not suffer the strange feelings I had in trying to map the new onto the old. And she enjoyed living in Central London for a while and going to the theatre and other things the capital has to offer.

The most difficult part of adapting to life in the UK was in actually getting anything done. We found that, compared with Hong Kong, the service sector was grossly inefficient, overpriced and unresponsive. The same was true at work. In Hong Kong, the entire building would shake on a direct command from the chairman as everyone leaped to carry it out. In the UK, a direct order from the chairman was often treated simply as an invitation to begin a discussion.

It was probably just as well my job at the Bank's new headquarters left little time for reflection. John Bond proved every bit as energetic, if quieter, than Willie Purves. Willie, who probably missed Hong Kong as much as any of us, said to me, 'If you are feeling down, the best response is hard work.' True no doubt, but that was Willie's answer to everything.

Under John's outstanding leadership, which marked a sea change in management style, the Bank prepared a strategic plan, consulting all the senior executives as it did so, then communicated it to all the staff, who by now numbered over 250,000. And then pursued it, relentlessly.

We bought banks in Mexico, Malta, Bermuda and France, the personal finance business of Household in the USA and, crucially, expanded our business in mainland China.

We created and promoted the HSBC brand and changed almost all the subsidiary names to conform to it. That was a great success despite some howls of protest from those companies that lost their names.

We listed the shares in New York (an achievement of particular satisfaction to John) and in Paris.

In five years we doubled the market capitalisation of the group and then embarked on another strategic plan aimed at achieving further growth.

Amongst all this frenzy of activity, one thing was starting to bother me. I wasn't feeling as good as I should. I had not felt 100 per cent for several years. This worry had emerged in Hong Kong in 1993 when I was in training for Trailwalker.

Sponsored by the Bank, this event involved teams of four, walking 100 km through the mountains and valleys of the New Territories within 24 hours. It was not for the faint-hearted but I believed that I was more than equal to it. David and I joined two of his colleagues to form a team and started training regularly, each Sunday tackling one or two stages. All went well until one not unusually hot day when I developed serious cramp. I struggled to complete that walk and tried again, but this time it was much worse.

I knew that I couldn't complete the course come the event itself. On the day I managed to complete stage 1 to allow my teammates to qualify to continue, and David and one other did complete the course.

Mortified, I went to see my GP who said it might be sunstroke or I might simply have the wrong body type for long distance. Having spent ten years tramping over the mountains and fells of Cumbria I thought he was talking nonsense.

Sadly, I was proved right. The period immediately before I began training for Trailwalker was to be the last time I ever felt completely well.

When Willie Purves visited Hong Kong, I returned the very generous cheque he had given me by way of sponsorship together with a note explaining that I would not be able to earn it after all. He came into my office almost straightaway and was most solicitous: 'If you have any serious concerns about your health, I want you to go and see a specialist here or get on a plane and go to London right away. The Bank will pay for whatever you need.'

This was a generous offer and typical of the man, but I declined it, saying I thought I had suffered only a case of heatstroke.

He looked at me doubtfully, gave me a stern lecture about looking after myself and strode out of the office, no doubt on his way to admonish someone else for a perceived shortcoming. Willie was a man who managed everyone and everything.

In this way I soldiered on for the rest of my time in Hong Kong and for six years in London. Inexorably the symptoms increased until I could no longer hide them: the tremor in the left hand; the painful left shoulder; the growing difficulty walking. I tried for as long as possible to ignore the symptoms and to deceive others. This became steadily more difficult.

For example, Luddite that I am, I continued to draft everything by hand using a Lamy ballpoint pen, which was thick enough to hold. But my handwriting became smaller and smaller and, hard though I tried to control it, increasingly illegible. It became difficult to hold a pen at all.

Thanks to Alyson and then Elaine, I managed to keep going, dictating everything either using shorthand or by sitting next to them as their enviably mobile fingers hammered away at the keyboard.

It was about this time that we drove down to Canterbury to see my elderly godmother, Betty Armitage. She, ever the tough hospital matron with the heart of gold, was the first person to speak up and say what others must have been thinking. As we were leaving, she asked quietly, 'Don't you think you should go and see a doctor?'

I said with genuine naivete, 'Why would I do that AB?'

She said firmly, 'Because of the tremor in your left hand; it is getting worse.'

My godmother was a shrewd woman and an excellent nurse. To her there was no doubt what was wrong with me. Also, she had seen the same symptoms in her mother forty years previously. No wonder she hugged me with unusual zeal when we parted that day. She had seen the future and knew what was in store for me.

By the beginning of 2004 my symptoms were becoming a serious problem and I was going to absurd lengths to hide them from Joyce and from my colleagues. My left shoulder was giving me constant pain and I had developed a pronounced limp. I don't suppose that I convinced anyone that I was fit when I had trouble putting on a jacket or a raincoat. Elaine always seemed to appear at just the right moment and help me. Discreet and intensely loyal as she was, she never asked what was wrong with me or passed comment.

Eventually in May 2004, right after my fiftieth birthday, I went to the BUPA Centre at work for a routine medical; height, weight, BMI, blood pressure and blood test, ECG, eyes, ears, nose, throat and then a confidential chat with a pleasant doctor with an agreeable (and expensive) bedside manner.

'So, Michael,' he began, 'you are the Bank's Director of Group Corporate Affairs. You must be a very important person with a title like that.'

So, I told him what the job involved.

'And would you say it's very stressful?' he asked kindly.

'It has its moments,' I answered airily; now slightly anxious about where we were headed with this conversation.

'In what way?' he pressed.

I replied, 'Well, in the first place it is extremely unpredictable; problems can and do come at you from anywhere and everywhere. You have virtually no control of your own life and work. You may plan to do something substantive one day and come into work all ready to start it, and then at 08.02 someone very senior rings you up and says, "We've got a problem, what are you going to do about it?" And that's your day gone. Or your week. Or your month. So the job is relentlessly contingent. Some of what you do in the role is very public and, if you screw up and get even one word wrong, the whole world knows. It could be very damaging to HSBC's reputation and very public. Also, the sheer volume of work passing through the department is a pressure. So yes, I would say it's stressful, but many people have jobs which are stressful.'

The good doctor observed, 'You are somewhat overweight.'

'That may well be true,' I countered, 'but with all due respect, doctor, your profession has been telling me that since I was twenty-two and I can assure you that at that age, and until I was thirty, I didn't have an ounce of fat on me. I am just a big man with a big frame and heavy bones. And at one time I had a lot of muscle although I will concede that there has been some redistribution in recent years.'

The doctor smiled indulgently. 'In most respects you are in excellent physical shape for a man of your age. But there is one thing that bothers me a good deal – the tremor in your hands, particularly the left.'

'Oh,' I replied, less airily now, 'I have noticed it too, I drink far too much coffee.'

The doctor looked at me kindly, 'Michael, I don't think coffee is your problem. I am sorry to have to tell you that I believe you are in the early stages of Parkinson's Disease.'

The doctor's pronouncement came as a shock but not a major one. I had known for some time that there was something wrong with me, but I had pushed it constantly to the back of my mind. In a way, it was a relief to be able to give it a name. Also, I knew almost nothing about the disease at that time and did not (or did not wish to) recognise it as a serious condition.

The BUPA doctor referred me to a colleague of his at the Lister Hospital in Chelsea, where I was given a scan. This involved being fed into a complicated machine that looked like an electronic doughnut designed by a committee.

Afterwards, a pleasant young Scotsman called Dr Innes showed me an alarming picture of the inside of my head. 'The bad news,' he announced (a little too cheerfully I thought), 'is that the scan confirms Parkinson's. The good news is that there are many different kinds and you have the most common one. And it is treatable with drugs, although these do wear off and lose their effectiveness after about five years and that has to be managed.' Then more quietly, he asked, 'Are you OK? How do you feel about that?'

I said, 'Well, doctor, no-one could call it good news, but if you told me that I had only six months to live, I would feel a lot worse.'

Dr Innes said, 'Goodness me, no, it's nothing like that. You are going to be all right'

I left the hospital in a reflective mood, feeling low but not deeply depressed. I thought, well now at least I know what's wrong with me. Sooner or later everyone gets something wrong with them.

I went home and told Joyce and she reacted calmly as I had done. Neither of us knew much about Parkinson's and we both thought there were worse things in life than an annoying tremor.

I have always made it a rule not to read about illness on the Internet (not even apparently authoritative websites). I do not trust the provenance of most of the information. Instead, I bought a couple of books on the subject and Joyce did the same.

I might as well have used the Internet. The books made chilling reading in their descriptions of what happens to the victims in the later stages.

I wondered how the descriptions of Parkinson's in the books squared with Dr Innes' assertion that I was going to be all right.

I discovered that there are two main types of PD but with as many different variations as there are patients.

One type involves steadily increasing dyskinesia, or shaking; the actor Michael J. Fox is a famous example of this.

The other involves growing periods of freezing or immobility and leads eventually to paralysis.

One is known by sufferers with a black sense of humour as the tumble drier, the other as the fridge freezer. I include myself in the second category although from time to time I have a severe tremor.

Both types are usually classified as 'idiopathic,' an impressive word that means that no one has a clue what caused them.

Other symptoms include breathing difficulties, impairment or loss of speech, difficulty swallowing and sleeping.

Possible causes include genetic factors, pesticides, concussion, and infantile trauma. As an adopted, ex rugby player my ears pricked up at the last two.

Initially in denial of the disaster that had struck us and reluctant to accept Dr Innes' diagnosis, we decided to seek a second opinion. We asked around to see who the leading authority in the country was. The name of Professor Neil Quinn kept coming up, so we made an appointment to see him.

It took several months to get to see the great man, but eventually we were given an hour at the National Hospital for Neurology in Queen Square. Professor Quinn was about to retire and seemed fairly demob happy; even though we were private patients he kept us waiting for an hour and offered no apology. I had arranged for my scan results to be sent to him in advance.

'Yes, I've looked at your scan and you do have idiopathic Parkinson's,' he said, 'but it's not usually fatal. There are some effective drugs available nowadays and the best way to see it is as just a damn nuisance. The important thing is to keep a positive attitude.'

I saw him a few times after that and then felt it was time to move on. I think by then he had said all he could usefully say.

I started to have outpatient consultations at the Charing Cross Hospital, which has a formal relationship with Imperial College. This choice was on the recommendation of my GP, though it struck us as odd, since we lived a few minutes' drive from St George's Hospital with its highly rated Atkinson Morley neurology department.

By early 2004, my symptoms were becoming too obvious even to delude myself that I could hide the condition any longer. And the exhaustion that accompanies PD was beginning to affect my work. I went to see HSBC's head of human resources, Connal Rankin, who I had known and liked for many years.

I told him about my problem and said that I might have to resign.

He said that he had suspected that all was not well and was extraordinarily sympathetic. He immediately set about checking what I might be entitled to in such circumstances.

A few days later I went to see John Bond and, at the end of our meeting about work-related matters, I told him I needed to tell him something of a personal nature. He got up from behind his desk and shut the door to his office. 'Go ahead,' he said.

'Chairman,' I replied, 'I have Parkinson's Disease and I may have to retire early.'

He looked visibly shocked and after a long pause said, 'Michael, I am so sorry. We never know what's around the corner. We will of course give you every possible support and you must tell us when you have had enough. And if you need to go somewhere, America, Switzerland for example, to get special treatment, the Bank will happily pay all your expenses.'

I was by then a senior executive who had given twenty years of his life to the Bank. I think I had done a reasonable job, sometimes in difficult circumstances. Nevertheless, the warmth and humanity of the response from a man who headed an organization, which by then numbered 330,000 people, was absolutely outstanding. And, thereafter, the concern and consideration that he, Stephen Green, and other senior executives showed to me, spoke volumes for the individuals and for the character of the institution. Despite its growth in size and the inevitable shift in culture caused by the move of the Group Head Office to London, HSBC at the very summit retained the values that had been such a salient feature of the Bank in Hong Kong.

In 2006, two years after the disclosure of my condition to John Bond and Stephen, I felt that the time had come to retire at the same time as John. I attended his final act as Group Chairman, which was to preside over that year's AGM at the Barbican.

At the end of the meeting, during which there was markedly less of the kind of hostile questioning which is often a feature of London AGMs, John was given a long and richly deserved standing ovation.

As I left the Barbican for the last time, I thought to myself that if the shareholders really knew how he had combined making very tough decisions with integrity, respect for his colleagues, customers and them, they would have applauded even longer.

And so it was that, after some thirty years working, some of them punishing, but at least a decade before I had expected, I suddenly found myself a gentleman of leisure with time – too much time – to reflect on my past and likely future.

I looked back at the golden age of Cambridge and the second, much longer one, in Hong Kong. I thought about my career and concluded that I had not really had one. Instead, not fitting any particular mould, I had enjoyed a calculated drift in the right direction. It had not worked out too badly, after all; I could look back with a degree of satisfaction. But the future was something altogether different. I did not know how many years I had left nor of what quality. I resolved to press on taking one day at a time and let what would happen, happen.

My departure from HSBC had been considerate and honourable. We parted on the best possible terms. Inevitably, however, it had also been quite abrupt. One moment I was in the hot seat, the next I was gone. There had been almost no time to prepare for retirement.

I didn't have any hobbies as such. Many people – at least many of those who can afford to – like to spend time travelling in their retirement. But travel for me was already hard and getting harder because of my restricted mobility. The last trip I had made on behalf of the Bank had been to Bermuda, and I had struggled with cramp and fatigue all the way there and all the way back.

Also, I had already been fortunate enough to see most of the world I wanted see. In my twenties and thirties I had a voracious appetite for travel and was impatient for the next airport and the next long-distance flight; by the time I was fifty I was largely satiated. Much of the fun had been lost and apart from forays into the more attractive parts of Europe, I preferred to be at home. This required an adjustment by Joyce, who continued to pursue a successful counselling career from home. Having grown used to a husband who was almost never there, she had to adapt to having one in the house almost constantly and loitering without intent.

As my 53rd birthday approached I felt I was at a crossroads. What was it to be; Thebes or Corinth? Either accept the inevitable, become a recluse and wait to die, or fight the cursed thing all the way up, knowing full well that there could only ever be one outcome, but that at least I would have tried. I decided that the struggle to survive would define me. The obvious first step was to master my fear and to stay positive. This required an act of will.

I started to read again, almost as voraciously as I had as a student, except this time my chosen subject was modern history. I read about five books a week for the first three years after leaving the Bank. I was now an autodidact, with no equivalent of Stephen Heath to guide me. Nevertheless, I told myself by the end of that period, that if I had enrolled in a formal course I could have come away with at least a 2:1.

During this period, I also wrote a novel. It had a beginning, a middle and, somewhat to my surprise, an end, as I hung on doggedly and just managed to finish it. Sadly, I knew it was not good; it proved conclusively that I simply lacked the talent and the creativity. If you wanted a speech written, or a press statement, or a letter to a finance minister, or a paper to the HSBC board or a communication to 330,000 staff, I was amongst the best. However, while the idea of waking early in the Dordogne or Siena and writing the great novel while infused with the creative muse was appealing, it remained just that, an appealing idea.

As it was, I had enjoyed my years with the Bank for the insider's perspective it conferred on current affairs and on economics and finance, for the enjoyment and the camaraderie of tackling major issues or problems and taking initiatives as part of a team. Also, my need for recognition was served by being known as someone who had the ear of the chairman, who was a trusted adviser and who got things done. All this I missed, for a while.

The dogs may bark but the caravan moves on. Free from the daily grind of going to work, I very much enjoyed the additional time I could spend with close friends. The keen awareness that time was running out made me more open and them more affectionate; it deepened our friendships. The trips we took together may have been conceived of originally as material for a book, and indeed, as we travelled round Europe with friends I learned a great deal. Nevertheless, the greatest pleasure was simply being with Anthony or Glen or John.

We visited Arras, Krakow, Barcelona, Berlin, Biarritz, Ypres, Waterloo, the D-Day landing beaches and the monuments and cemeteries of the Western Front. We improved our minds but we also had a good deal of fun. To a man they were unfailingly patient and tolerant of my condition even when it became necessary to use a wheelchair.

In addition to renewing old friendships I made some new ones, notably Tom and Kate Huckin. I had known them for many years but principally as close friends of Peter and Lizzie Dix. Now I had the opportunity to get to know them much better. We were by then firmly established in Wimbledon where they had lived for many years. Tom and I used to meet up regularly, mainly to talk about rugby and the more I saw him and Kate the more I liked them. Tom and I had something else in common, a growing list of health problems. Over time our conversation became less concerned with the state of the England rugby team and more about which ailment was the current preoccupation. So dominant did this theme become that we renamed our get togethers for morning coffee or afternoon tea 'The Organ Recitals'.

Jola (later our carer) once observed that when a person becomes ill, some of their 'friends' disappear quite quickly because illness is ugly and because they do not wish to be reminded of their own mortality. 'But Michael' she said, 'Your friends are different; they draw closer as if to protect you'.

Although one friend did fall blatantly by the wayside and others showed varying degrees of empathy, the core circle of friends became even more supportive.

There was no single date for the tipping point when things became really difficult. However, in the summer of 2015 and after much debate, Joyce and I went on a short cruise on the Cunard *Queen Victoria* up the Norwegian fjords. It was our Silver Wedding that year, and that was the only reason we needed for travelling first class in a big stateroom with a big balcony and every conceivable luxury. I remember thinking I had come a long way from trying to get some sleep as John Moore and I lay on platform 1 at Narbonne station.

I had been reluctant go on the cruise because of what other people had told me about them. I thought that there would be too much holiday camp jollity and too much compulsory singing. In fact, we had a wonderful time; it was one of the best holidays we ever had as well as the most expensive. We enjoyed the stunningly beautiful fjords in magnificent weather, the like of which the captain said he had not seen in thirty years of sailing.

I felt surprisingly well. I was able to walk round the deck of the ship several times a day which, given the amount we had to eat and drink, was a necessity. We were very happy in each other's company and lived for the moment, largely oblivious to the storm clouds that were gathering.

With hindsight the Norwegian cruise marked a watershed for us. Before it life, though circumscribed by my illness, was still tolerable. I had already enjoyed almost a decade of reasonably comfortable retirement.

Notwithstanding the assurance of the experts at Charing Cross Hospital that Parkinson's develops slowly and that I would not suffer a sudden and violent decline, by the autumn of that year my health had taken a marked turn for the worse. What in the summer had been relatively minor problems – sleeping, swallowing, walking, talking – had all worsened. I was suffering from an increasing number of freezing spells and each was becoming longer. It appeared that, slightly later than the average schedule, the medication I had been taking had begun to wear off.

We grew increasingly anxious about how we were going to cope.

It so happened that the year before, the local medical practice had closed. My GP, a deeply unimpressive man with fixed ideas based largely on personal prejudice and surprisingly little medical knowledge, chose to retire. With relief, I registered with a new GP up in Wimbledon Village.

I too have personal prejudices and one of them is in favour of female GPs. In my experience women are innately better suited than men to the front line of the caring professions.

I went to see Dr Rutter and asked if it would be possible to get a second opinion. My previous GP had assured me that the NHS did not allow them but I now believe he was simply too idle to be bothered to write a letter referring me to another neurologist. She said of course I could, and expressed surprise that my previous GP had sent me to the Charing Cross Hospital when my home address fell squarely in the area covered by St George's. Clucking with disapproval at the way I had been treated, she was profoundly kind and sympathetic when (as if to back up my claims) I suffered a major freeze that kept me in her consulting room for almost three hours.

The next day she wrote a letter referring me to the head of neurology at St George's Hospital in Tooting.

I had my first appointment there in the spring of 2014. It was with the chief Parkinson's nurse, Alison Leake, and I began by summarising the history of my condition and the treatment I had so far received. 'Furthermore,' I said, 'Dr Rutter has said that you have a team of people who do home visits and give practical advice on modifying one's home to make life easier for PD sufferers.'

'That's correct,' replied Alison. 'However, there is something much more important I would like to discuss with you now. We have just started trials of a new drug for Parkinson's patients. It is called apomorphine and it is being tested in four centres in Britain – London, Oxford, Cambridge and Manchester – with a view to securing approval for general use by the NHS. We are looking for volunteers and I wonder if you would consider being one. It is quite time-consuming but I see you are retired.'

'Why not,' I said airily 'let's give it a whirl. As the man said, I'll try anything once except incest and Morris dancing.'

Alison looked at me quizzically. I could tell that she did not think it was a matter to make jokes about. 'Thank you,' she said, 'the next step will be for you to come back for a full medical examination and a meeting with the head of the project, Dr Dominic Paviour.'

Two weeks later I was back in St George's being examined for my suitability to stand trial. A tall blonde nurse who introduced herself as Ruth weighed me, measured me, tested my blood pressure, gave me an ECG, took my temperature and extracted what seemed to be about three litres of blood with which she filled numerous phials. 'This reminds me of working for HSBC,' I said facetiously.

'We take your bloods,' she answered (I always found the plural slightly unsettling), 'and send them to the laboratory to test for a wide variety of conditions.'

Before I could ask any more questions, the door opened and Alison came in followed by a tall, slim, fit-looking man in his early forties. 'This is Dr Paviour,' she announced, a hint of reverence in her voice.

We shook hands and he asked me to sit down. Then he asked me a number of questions about my history, my present condition, the seriousness of my symptoms and my current and rather complicated medication. He struck me initially as a very serious man, earnest to a fault, reserved if not cold. And it was clear that the others in the room were in awe of him. He thanked me for agreeing to take part in the trial. 'I don't know how much you know about apomorphine,' he said. 'It is not a new drug, it was developed in the 1960s as a treatment for celebrity heroin addicts, people like Keith Richards and the writer William Burroughs'.

'Sounds like my kind of drug,' I said, and this elicited a hint of a smile.

'It was discovered almost by accident to have a beneficial effect on some Parkinson's patients and then found to be more effective if taken subcutaneously and pumped in continuously. The purpose of this trial, which is sponsored by the manufacturers, is to obtain NHS approval and thus make it widely available in this country and internationally accepted.'

'So, this is a British invention? Is apomorphine produced in the UK too?' I asked.

'It is British,' he replied, 'but it is produced in Germany, why do you ask?'

'Security of supply,' I answered, 'one of the basic rules of warfare.'

He laughed at this and the atmosphere became noticeably warmer. He explained that the trial would be conducted blind, that is to say some patients would be given the drug and some a placebo; none of the patients or the doctors or the nurses would know, so that no other influences could affect the outcome. 'It is remarkable how powerful the mind can be,' explained Dr Paviour. 'Some of the best results we have had with apomorphine and other drugs have been with people actually on placebos.'

And so it was that I embarked on my new career as a laboratory rat (which some friends kindly observed was a step up). For two weeks I went to St George's all day, every day.

On the first morning I was given nine questionnaires to complete, covering every possible aspect of my personal life. Tellingly, the first questionnaire was about suicide; Dr Paviour himself completed it. The first question was, 'Have you ever considered it.'

'Yes,' I admitted, 'in the months after Cambridge it did cross my mind. I thought at the time that it was due to overwork as a student and that I had pushed myself to the limits. But later I concluded that it wasn't that at all. It was more like Schopenhauer's concept of being adrift in a rudderless boat on an unknown sea. The red carpet that was supposed to await people with upper Firsts from Cambridge had been rolled up and was nowhere to be seen.'

'And what did you do about your depression?' Dr Paviour asked quietly.

'I went to see my GP and tried to explain to him what was going on in my head. And he was utterly unsympathetic, totally useless. He was unworthy of the title doctor. So, I went out and drank too much and did a lot of other things that I shouldn't have done. I got married when I knew it was a mistake. We divorced quickly and then I was on my own. I saw a lot of some of my old Cambridge friends but they were all

241

making their way in the world and seemed to know where they were going. My depression continued, albeit on and off and on a lower level, for the next nine years'

'And then what happened?' Dr Paviour asked.

'I went to Hong Kong and lived happily ever after,' I said and everyone laughed. And it had been true. One day I had boarded a plane at Gatwick and some fourteen hours later I emerged into the sunshine of Hong Kong – a man reborn. That first journey of little more than half a day was worth seven years of lying on a psychiatrist's couch. Hong Kong kick-started my life which had been heading nowhere.

'I see,' said Dr Paviour and I knew that he did. 'And since that time, you have not been depressed not even when you were told you had Parkinson's?'

'I have felt down sometimes since my diagnosis I must admit,' I said, 'but suicidal? No. It is another of life's challenges and I am a fighter, so I will struggle. If you can meet with Triumph and Disaster and treat those two imposters just the same... etc. etc.'

Later that day, they showed me how the apomorphine pump worked. It was an odd-looking device consisting of a small metal box on top of which was attached a plastic phial containing the drug. On that was a slim plastic tube that ended in a clip. Then, taking a small blue cartridge, you pushed it hard against your stomach. You lifted the cartridge case leaving the needle, hopefully, stuck firmly in the skin and you attached the tube. Then, having set the required flow, you were ready to go. If it sounds complicated, it is, or rather it was initially, but I soon became expert and after a few weeks could do it blindfold, which I once did literally, just to prove that I could.

On the first day of the trial they stuck a needle in me and we waited. And waited. And waited. I sat in the room in the hospital with Ruth, the blonde nurse who turned out to be not quite so cool after all, and was pleasant company and with James, a hulking male nurse who shared my passion for rugby. Every day, twice a day, they turned up the flow rate in the pump and still nothing happened.

Suddenly, just after lunch on the Thursday of that first week, I had a strange sensation. I felt as though I was being inflated and all of a sudden was floating on air, walking about free of pain and with an ease that I had not felt in ten years. I was moving freely and easily. 'Eureka. We have lift off!' I shouted. 'They are not firing blanks into me, it's working.'

Ruth came into the room and saw the look on my face. 'How does it feel?' she said.

'Bloody marvellous,' I answered. 'I feel twenty years younger.'

In my excitement I called Joyce to tell her the good news and also John Moore because I knew he was waiting to hear from me. But then, with hideous cruelty, after about forty minutes, the feeling drained away and did not return.

I waited the rest of that day and all of the next and the whole of the following week, hour after hour, day after day and still the feeling did not return. Dr Paviour was at a loss to explain it.

The following week they put the pump on me again and stuck the needle in my stomach but this time they knew they were using live ammunition.

'We will start you on 1 ml per hour,' Dr Paviour said, 'because you are a big, strong man and you tell me that you need much higher doses of medication than most people.'

I spent the rest of the day at that level and the next morning too. Nothing happened.

'OK,' said Dr Paviour, 'let's take it up to 1.1. '

Nothing.

A day later he said with a touch of exasperation, '1.2, that's the highest dosage anyone has needed so far.'

Nothing.

1.3 nothing.

1.4 nothing.

And after he had left the room, I asked Ruth, 'Do you happen to know if they plan to bring out a version of this medicine for adults?'

'You are showing off,' she said.

1.5 nothing.

1.6 is the limit imposed by the trial protocol; Alison is now involved and looking worried. 'We really can't go any higher Michael.'

'Why not?' I ask.

'Well, because there might be side effects,' Alison says.

I say, 'Surely the time to worry about side effects is when the drug starts to have any effect at all.'

Alison agrees that I have a point and so we continue.

1.7 nothing.

Finally, at 1.8 the drug kicks in and I begin to enjoy the extra mobility and the comfort that apomorphine provides, albeit nowhere near as extraordinary as the experience the previous week. Unofficially, Dr Paviour says that I have the highest dosage of anyone involved in the trial.

'Dura virum nutrix,' I say to myself.

Chapter 10 - Things Fall Apart

'If we had a keen vision and feeling of all ordinary human life, it would be like hearing the grass grow or listening to the squirrel's heartbeat, and we should die of that roar which lies on the other side of silence. As it is, the quickest of us walk about well wadded with stupidity.' George Eliot, *Middlemarch*

As time went by my condition grew worse, I spent an increasing amount of time in my bedroom sitting in an armchair and I became morose and impatient. The frustration I felt at my inability to do anything and my need to crawl around the house on hand and knees because I could not stand up, must have been deeply depressing and unnerving.

Joyce and I began to quarrel. This was unusual for us because for most of our marriage we had been very happy together and had renewed our wedding vows in 2013. It reflected the tension caused by advancing Parkinson's Disease and the burden it placed on Joyce for doing more and more. It intruded into every area of our lives. There was no doubt that we still loved each other deeply, but the way we responded to my condition reflected two very different personalities.

Joyce has always said that she thinks in poetry and that I think in prose. She expressed her sense of mortality in these words:

The Gossamer Sweetness of Youth

Early one morning

Walking my dogs,

I saw a gentleman,

Tall, stooped, smiling,

With his lady companion.

I smiled.

What a loving couple.

He came every day

For a walk.

One day,

The companion was another woman.

In my innocence

I thought,

How strange.

Did his wife die

Replaced by another?

Today.

The gentleman

Is my husband,

The companion,

His carer.

Although Joyce had a successful career in business in Hong Kong, and is perfectly capable of pragmatism, and although she can be very practical, she is essentially a spiritual person. Her strong Christian faith is tempered only by her predominantly Buddhist family background. She has spent much of her life on her spiritual development. She is a Reiki Master, a keen student of meditation and mindfulness, and an avid reader of the literature of the soul.

Good Hong Kong girl that Joyce is, she does not believe it necessary to take Carmelite vows and to renounce all material things in order to enter heaven. She has no difficulty in reconciling faith with worldly wealth. Nevertheless, her guiding light is God not Mammon and remains troubled by the huge disparity between the rich and the poor in Hong Kong. She often felt uneasy about the more venal excesses of her home.

She is fiercely loyal to her husband, her siblings and her friends, and although sometimes is disappointed by what she sees as their failings and quick to criticise them, she is also quick to forgive. She has a keen instinct for any kind of racism. She is excitable, emotional, humorous, affectionate and kind.

This poem describes the contrast between her inner and outer world.

I. Am. Fine.

You ask me how I am.

The slow tortuous stream
Of anguish flows secretly.

Feel the undercurrent of sorrow,
Hear the bubbling babbling of fear,
Catch the blood of each splish splash,
Ricocheting mid-stream
Against each rock.

I put on my make-up
Smile at you
And say

'I'm fine.'

Learning to accept and cope with my slow but inexorable decline sent her on a rollercoaster of emotional turmoil. It plunged her into the depths of depression and back up to the crest of hope, then back down into despondency as the limitations of each initiative by my doctors become evident.

For much of my illness she has been kind and sympathetic but at times she has seemed brittle or indifferent or even hard. There have been times when she has seemed to be critical of everything I do. I believe this is when she is hurting and feeling the most and struggling hard to keep her emotions in check.

There have also been times since I became ill when she seemed to be succumbing to the pain – times when she has seemed overburdened by all the things she has to do for me. She arranges the hospital and GP appointments and ensures that the medications are in constant supply. The stress of all this has sometimes made her irascible and not her usual self. At such times I felt that I was walking on eggshells knowing that whatever I said would be wrong.

Occasionally, she has launched into a long tirade, criticising everything I have done or not done as a husband, how ungrateful and how thoughtless I am. She tells me that my illness has caused deterioration in her emotional health and physical health. I am sure it has.

There are times when I can hear in her voice a longing to be free. I understand. Living with someone with a long-term illness imposes an intolerable burden on many people.

Yet sometimes she is her old self, warm and openly affectionate.

Whatever her mood she has always done the right thing when it most mattered, whether it has involved getting me into a private hospital on New Year's Eve or bringing forward the timing of surgery so that I do not have it in winter.

This is how Joyce expressed it.

You Ask Too Much of Me

I drove down a road
Sliding into the abyss
Eyes trained on the headlight
Watching out for that small
Opening I call home.

When the fireworks hit the sky
Wayfarers in funny hats
Called out greetings of
Good cheer
I sit alone in the dead of night
Eating a microwaved meal.

You ask me to understand
What it's like to be you
Battling a degenerative disease

Testing limits
Testing mine.

Do you know what it's like
Fighting the system
For your life
For mine
Home from hospital
On New Year's Eve?

Without Joyce it is extremely unlikely that I would still be alive but it has come at a cost to her. There have been times when I have thought she really can hear the grass grow and listen to the squirrel's heartbeat. Joyce's problem has been not that she did not care but that she cared too much.

I, on the other hand, have for many years 'walked about well wadded with stupidity'. This, no doubt, partly the result of ten years of desensitizing boarding schools which teach you to endure pain and hardship without complaint.

In part it is the result of a conscious decision. I learned in my early twenties that constant brooding and thinking about the meaning of life and about my place in it had led me almost to the point of a nervous breakdown, but had provided no compensating insights or self-knowledge.

When I first became aware I had PD I did pass through a 'why me' phase, but concluded quickly that it was not a profitable line of enquiry and that the only possible response to the calamity was to fight like hell to maintain the best quality of life I could achieve, for as long as possible, for my own sake and for Joyce's. Beyond that point where further struggle is futile it seemed the only option was to accept it and, as a final act of defiance, to laugh at the absurdity of it all. As is my habit I turned to literature and to the best that has been thought and said on the subject. Amongst the spectrum of possible responses from Chaucer to Dostoyevsky, I found two that chimed with my own inclination. In Ernest Hemingway's great novel, *For whom the Bell Tolls*, Robert Jordan lies in extremis at the end of the book and 'tried not to think but only to endure', while in the same author's consummate *The Old Man and the Sea,* Santiago 'rested sitting on the unstepped mast and sail and tried not to think but only to endure'.

It is hard to imagine how difficult the last decade must have been on Joyce. It must be an immense strain on anyone to watch someone they love being destroyed slowly but surely by a degenerative disease. How much worse it is when you remember him as he was, a big, strong man who, you used to joke with your friends, you married for his biceps, and is now being gradually brought to his knees. It is worse still when you feel his pain acutely but you know there is next to nothing that you can do about it.

Since my retirement I had been in the habit of going out on my own in the afternoons two or three times a month. Joyce was seeing clients at home and it was partly to keep out of her way, partly because I felt the need to get out of the house, and partly because I did not know how much longer I would be able to leave the house on my own.

I used to enjoy these solitary trips. I would take the Underground and choose a station at random after a quick look at the maps at home. In this way I got to see many parts of London I would never have visited otherwise. The more I saw of the city the more I came to appreciate its extraordinary energy and its richness of sights and sounds. A hundred different villages and a hundred different communities live side by side, for the most part in harmony. London is far more cosmopolitan than Hong Kong, which is essentially a Chinese city. The more I saw of London the more I liked it – Wembley, Vauxhall, Hampstead, Fulham, Tooting, each with its own trades and cuisine, its own religion, its own mores, a hundred different communities in one massive city.

At the beginning, I used to get about quite easily, hopping on and off the tube with the naïve enthusiasm of a tourist. However, as time went by, life became more difficult. I suffered from freezing spells, rooted to the spot wherever I happened to be standing. The freezes started at several minutes, but became longer and longer until they could last several hours. There are a number of Underground stations where I have spent more time than I might have wished.

Joyce always worried about me going out on my own, and her anxiety grew in line with the increasing frequency of my late arrival for dinner following a lengthy freeze somewhere in the city. At the beginning she showed her relief, and later her relief and her irritation. But when I started coming home in police cars and ambulances, having been hauled off a street or a station platform and assessed as a danger to myself and the public, she drew the line, calling me irresponsible and selfish. From her point of view those were fair judgements. However, I protested in my defence that my outings were a necessary means of asserting a degree of independence and that staying at home all the time was a victory for the enemy.

Some of our friends said they thought I was courageous venturing out and ignoring the obvious risks.

Others, sympathetic to Joyce's concerns, thought I should accept defeat and stay at home. I was very reluctant to give up my local travel and pointed out that each and every time I found myself in difficulty, a good Samaritan had come to my rescue.

In fact, the reaction of Londoners to a man in obvious difficulty eventually led me to revise my views on mankind. I believe that this was a clear-headed appraisal but even so it was a revelation. I did not go to bed one night thinking all men and women were evil and wake up the next day knowing that all mankind was good.

It was true that most people walked straight past me, as though I were invisible. But the fact is that during six years of wandering round different parts of London, every time I froze, sooner or later someone always came to the rescue: male, female, Asian, Arab, black, white, old, young, rich, poor, Christian, Muslim. Almost everyone I met was kind, considerate and went out of their way to help me, by lending an arm to rest on or by summoning a taxi for me; because London – great, teeming, multi-cultural city that it is – is a microcosm of mankind. My view led me to a provisional conclusion that mankind is a more compassionate species than is often recognised. I am not sure that homo sapiens is naturally good and of course has an unenviable record of appalling behaviour. I am not in any sense Panglossian but if there are, say, only 200 really kind people in the world it would be a coincidence if they all lived in London.

On the whole, the view of mankind from the wheelchair is inspiring. I have had only three bad experiences since developing PD.

There was a waiter in a restaurant near L'Opèra in Paris who insisted on us leaving our table as soon as we had finished lunch, even though the place was half full. He was unbelievably rude and unpleasant even though we explained repeatedly that I was frozen. The gentleman at the table opposite looked deeply ashamed of his countryman and tried to intervene. When I had recovered sufficiently to leave, I remembered enough French to suggest what the waiter might usefully do with his table.

Then there were the members of staff at Cheltenham station who, in getting me off the train, showed such oafish incompetence and surly and patronising attitudes that we vowed never to go there by train again.

However, first prize must go to two well-dressed, middle-aged women who passed by me in Wimbledon while I was in a deep freeze and completely unable to move. They paused to look me up and down disapprovingly, muttered something about cleaning up the drunks and other human detritus from the streets and then proceeded into the nearby church. I wrote an account of this for my cousin Hugh, a clergyman in Kent, and I believe he turned it into a powerful sermon, using the Sadducees and Pharisees as the models for that kind of hypocrisy.

Eventually, the day came in the autumn of 2015, when enough was enough, even for me. I finally gave an undertaking to Joyce that there were to be no more solo expeditions. However, I obviously did not wish to stop all travel when I had company.

In December that year we went with John and Liz Moore to Cambridge. We had often talked about attending the carol service at King's College which by common consent is one of the finest such events in the world. It is also one of the most popular and we realised that our chances of ever getting tickets, for which members of the general public queued for many hours, were zero. We decided instead to attend the Jesus College service. There was novelty in this because in the three years we were undergraduates neither John nor I had ever set foot in the chapel. I had been in there once, as an usher for the wedding of Peter and Lizzie Dix, which took place the year after graduation.

About a week before the carol service, I had woken one morning with a severe pain in the middle of my chest. At first, I thought I was having a heart attack, but when I turned on my side the pain, which was excruciating, followed it and now my side was agony. And when I turned to the other side the pain followed it again. I had no idea what it was but I knew immediately it was serious. An idea occurred to me simultaneously. This was my way out. I would do nothing but let nature take its course by not seeking any medical assistance and letting whatever it was put me out of my misery. It would be the perfect crime and no responsibility could be laid at the door of Joyce, my GP or anyone else. And I would save the cost of an airfare to Zurich. So, for the next week or so I moved around very gingerly, grimacing sometimes as the pain bit fiercely. Then, as planned, we met up with John and Liz and took the train to Cambridge. As far as I could, I behaved as though I was suffering no more than usual.

John was as solicitous as ever and, although he insisted that he really enjoyed the weekend, I felt badly about using him to help maintain the illusion of normality. The poor man seemed to be spending an inordinate amount of time pushing my wheelchair to various parts of the college and tracking down elusive Cambridge taxis in the pouring rain. As things turned out we fared pretty well.

After a pleasant and unscheduled meeting with Rod Mengham, we set out for dinner on Magdalene Bridge and then returned to the Jesus College guest rooms I had booked.

I was not feeling well and opted to have a rest during the first part of the carol service. However John, Liz and Joyce came back for me during the intermission and I returned for the second half, which included splendid renditions of several of my favourite carols. For a brief moment I forgot my diseased and dying body and was carried away by the beauty of the chapel. I came as close as I shall get to a spiritual experience and afterwards John, Liz and Joyce said they had felt something similar. That alone made the struggle of travelling to Cambridge worthwhile. I do not expect to have the same experience again.

A few days later, our good friend Chris Bale came for lunch and as usual we talked about the things that interested us, both trivial and not so trivial. Towards the end of lunch, I began to feel really unwell and about an hour after Chris had left, I collapsed in my bedroom in great pain.

Joyce called for a doctor straight away and to his credit Peter Milton, our GP at the time, came immediately. He examined me briefly and called for an ambulance. One came quickly and I was taken to the grossly overworked Accident and Emergency Department of St George's Hospital in Tooting. Here, after a ghastly four-hour wait during which a drug addict unnerved everyone by screaming endlessly, I was finally given some attention.

I was taken initially into a high dependency unit. Two things stand out clearly in my memory from this process.

The first was that when I was moved from the gurney onto the X-ray table, I howled in agony and one of two middle-aged Irish nurses said to me, without a trace of sympathy, 'Michael, can you keep quiet? This is not much fun for us either, you know.'

I remember thinking, 'You bitch, you bloody bitch. If I survive this I am going to get you fired. You are not fit to be with people.'

The second probably took place while I was waiting for a CT scan, but I cannot be sure because I was half conscious and racked with pain. This was a bizarre debate I had with myself as two quite separate people.

One said in a voice I could recognise easily as my own, 'Come on Mike, congratulations! Success! Your plan has worked. You have what you wanted. All you have to do now is to shut the door behind you and it will all be over. You will be able to relax. No more pain, no more humiliation. You will be able to stop playing the tough guy. All your troubles will be at an end. Go, man, go for it, this is what you have been hoping for. This is what you have been planning. This is your big chance!'

But then my other voice, just as clearly my own but sounding most indignant, spoke up, 'Look. Don't listen to this nonsense. Sure, it hurts now but this is what you were bred for. You pride yourself in being a fighter, so stand up and fight this bastard.'

I have no idea what caused this spirited debate, whether it was a dream, a hallucination, a chimaera induced by painkillers or a quarrel between my conscious mind and my unconscious. But it was a very vivid part of me desperately wanting to shut down and take advantage of this opportunity for an organic suicide, while the other voice sounded like a curmudgeonly Yorkshireman, bloody-minded, rebellious, scornful of edicts and anything that spoke of weakness.

After this argument had raged in my head for several minutes or was it really seconds (or hundredths of a second?), the part of me that wanted to die gave up and said, 'OK. Have it your way you obstinate sod. Fight if you must but you were the one who wanted it all to end, remember? So, don't blame me if it hurts like hell. You were right on the edge of achieving your goal. Bloody fool, go and fight if you must.'

And so I chose life, and I fought and it hurt like hell but I won. I won.

After the witches of the high dependency unit had finished 'caring' for me I was transferred to the Intensive Care Unit or Intensive Treatment Unit (ITU), and even in my weakened state I could sense a very different atmosphere. It was almost as if I had moved to a different hospital.

The ITU was quiet, the staff moved around carefully and with calm intent.

Soon a very charming lady doctor came to see me. She knelt down by my bed and patted my arm reassuringly. 'How are you feeling, Michael?' she asked.

'Never better, doctor,' I croaked.

She smiled at me indulgently. 'Do you know where you are?'

'I believe I am in the ITU at St George's Hospital in Tooting,' I said with confidence.

'You know you are very ill,' she said.

'I figured there must be some reason why I'm in here,' I replied.

'We are going to do everything we can to help you,' she said, 'but I have to tell you it's not going to be easy.'

'That's fine,' I said, 'I know that you will give it your best shot.'

She said, 'You have a massive chest infection. We are going to try to drain your chest but if we cannot do so we would need to perform major surgery and that would mean general anaesthetic.'

'Understood,' I said, for some reason unable to think of a witty riposte.

'And if we do that,' she continued, 'there is a possibility that you might not wake up naturally, so I have to ask you, if that happens, do you want to be resuscitated?'

'No way,' I say, 'absolutely not. When it's over it's over and I have no problem with that.'

I wondered how many times she had had this conversation with ITU patients, but she looked as if she had not begun to get used to it. There were tears in her eyes.

'Thank you, Michael, we are sure you are going to be fine; but just in case we had to ask.'

I saw her write DNR (Do Not Resuscitate) on the form she was holding. Then she squeezed my hand and wished me well and then she went away. How anyone with so much compassion could do a job like that I did not know but I felt reassured.

I can no longer remember the exact sequence of events after that, but Joyce came to see me and we had a short and rather stilted conversation and I knew she was trying desperately hard to be strong for me.

And then Tom Pearson visited me on Christmas Eve having got on the first train from Basingstoke as soon as he heard the news. We talked a little about what had happened and even in my weakened state I recognised his demonstration of true friendship.

John Moore wanted to come down from Merseyside but on Christmas Eve there was a strong possibility that he might not get back for Christmas with his family and at my insistence Joyce implored him to stay put.

A little time later, after I had slept for a while, they began the process by which they hoped to save my life. They gave me a local anaesthetic and then drilled two holes in my chest. Then they paused and examined my scan and then they drilled a third hole because they discovered that the first hole was not in the right place.

They then produced some lengths of what I was convinced were garden hose and they attached one end to me and the other end to a tank. And they explained that they were going to inject a cleansing agent into my chest until the pressure forced all the poison out. All quite simple I thought, but there was a catch.

The doctor told me that the infection was not in one place, so I shouldn't think of it as a pool of water that had to be emptied. It had seeped all over my upper body and that they were therefore obliged to turn me from one side to the other so that the cleaning agent reached every nook and cranny.

I said that I understood, which I did, not least because I had spent five years with Shell and it sounded similar to the techniques used in extracting crude oil from certain types of wells.

The first hour of injecting cleaning agent seemed quite tolerable, but when it came time to turn me on my chest with the hoses still in place it took me to a level of pain that I never knew existed. They gave me morphine but in totally inadequate quantities.

By the next morning when they had moved me a dozen times, I asked them to kill me rather than continue with this torture any longer.

For a while life hung by a thread.

For two days, my life expectancy was measured in hours rather than days. The crisis reached its peak on Christmas Day and Joyce, who had been to see me, was invited to go home to wait for the telephone call to tell her she was now a widow.

But somehow I survived, and after two days of excruciating pain they told me that there was no longer any need to turn me and that the crisis had passed. I began to feel a little stronger, had little pain and began to eat and drink again.

The ITU nurses were first rate, especially the two young blonde Irish girls who had clearly found their true vocation. They could not have been more different to the harridans who had shown so little kindness the night I had arrived. I asked them if they were paid a lot extra for working in the ITU. They said not, and I was appalled when one of them told me what she was paid.

I found the hospital food unappetising and so I lived on high protein drinks for most of the time I spent in St George's.

As a major teaching hospital, the head of the ITU would bring groups of students round when not dealing with an immediate crisis. He would spend a few minutes talking with each patient before making some general comments about their condition. He stopped with his group of students when he reached my bed and examined the charts on the clipboard.

'How are you today?' he asked.

'Much better, thanks,' I replied, 'although it is a relief to have the garden hoses removed.'

He said, 'Michael, we were very worried about you when you first came in'.

Turning to his students he described my condition when I entered the hospital and the process by which they cleaned out my chest. Then, turning back to me again he said, 'We drained 4.5 litres of noxious fluid from you, and I have to say I have never seen another human being who could survive that amount of poison in him, never mind walk and talk as you have done.'

Utterly exhausted as I was, I managed a weak smile. 'Well, doctor,' I said, 'you have obviously never been to the Hong Kong Rugby Sevens.' And that drew laughter from the doctor and his students.

Thereafter, when any one of them passed my bed I was rewarded with a smile or a thumbs-up, proving that God and the medical profession help those who help themselves.

Soon after that I was declared to be off the danger list and well enough to be transferred to a ward. This was presented to me as a giant step forward. It was nothing of the sort. It was a huge step back.

Marnham Ward was crammed full of people with terrible respiratory problems, most of them dying. The ward was run by nurses who did not appear to give a damn and none of them had any knowledge of Parkinson's. They confiscated all my medication and refused to take any notice of my detailed medication regime. The ward was full of noise and of alarms going off all night to which no one appeared to pay the slightest attention. In short, it was a vision of hell, as Joyce agreed when she came to see me.

I told her that I had to get out of there as soon as possible, even if it meant going home.

To this day I do not know how she managed to fight her way through the bureaucracy, especially on that most difficult day of the year on which to get anything done, New Year's Eve, but she came and extracted me from St George's and took me to the private Parkside Hospital. In achieving this remarkable feat, she was accompanied and supported magnificently by Sim Comfort, a friend and neighbour whose wife had died on the bed next to mine in the same ward (although we did not discover that until later).

I stayed in Parkside for ten days recuperating before being allowed home.

Thus we entered 2016, bruised but not broken, bloodied but unbowed.

'I am sorry to tell you that you will not see another Christmas.' Dr Milton sat opposite, his big brown desk a barrier between us. I had gone to see him two weeks after I came home from Parkside and we had a long talk about the future.

'How do you feel in yourself?' he asked.

'Pretty low,' I said. 'I thought advanced PD was enough to be getting on with, but throw in a touch of pneumonia and you really are in trouble.'

He said, 'That, sadly, is what I have to tell you.' I was sure he really did feel sad. 'The problem is that you've had two serious illnesses which together would destroy the strongest of men. The long-term effects of Parkinson's exhaust you because they require so much effort to go on living. Then, when the pneumonia strikes, the double blow is just too much for anyone to handle. I can see that you are exhausted, absolutely spent and I'm afraid you will just run out of reserves and stop. Like a car running out of petrol,' he added helpfully.

'How certain can you be about this?' I asked.

'I am absolutely certain; there is nothing else I can do for you,' he replied.

We sat in silence for a moment.

Then I said, 'May I ask a favour? When the time comes, will you come to my house and put me out of my misery?'

He answered, 'Michael, you know that I am not allowed to do that but I can promise that I will do everything I can do to ease the way.'

I stared at the floor for a moment then looked up at Dr Milton. I suddenly felt angry. 'My life has been destroyed by Parkinson's. I may have done some bad things and deserve some kind of retribution, but what has Joyce done to deserve having her life torn apart in this brutal way? Nothing, absolutely nothing. I tell you, I cannot see the hand of God in any of this.'

'Nor can I, Michael,' replied Dr Milton.

As far as I could see, Peter Milton was an experienced GP with a wealth of knowledge to draw on. I thanked him for his candour (rare amongst doctors) and asked if he would come round to my house and break the news to Joyce. I felt it would be less emotional, and more objective, more scientific if she heard the news from a professional. And it would leave no room for the possibility of doubt, no scrabbling over semantics to try to find the ambiguity that might leave a trace of false hope. Dr Milton did come round to our house and he did tell Joyce exactly he had told me. She took the news calmly enough, and if she shed tears that evening she shed them in private.

I prepared for the last year of my life with thoroughness. After Dr Milton's visit I spent the next few

271

weeks simply waiting to die. We had both taken his visit as an accurate assessment and this was supported by the way I was feeling. I was so low that I felt sure it couldn't take more than a few weeks or a maximum of three months.

We told a few close friends about the doctor's prognosis and, inevitably, soon everyone knew. I was very touched by the large number of people who came ostensibly to say hello but really to say goodbye. Friends, old and new, close and not so close, former colleagues, faces half remembered. They all trooped past. It lifted my spirits to think that I might have achieved much in my own life but that at least I had touched a few others in a positive way.

There were so many visitors from February to April 2016 that I called this period my lying in state, and drew a satirical comparison with the death of Lenin.

Throughout this period, Joyce played the perfect hostess, greeting visitors, supplying food and drinks, seeing them out again when the conversation at last faltered. Privately, though, it was a huge strain for her and she was relieved when in June we called a halt and sent out what was I hope a polite note declining further visitors.

I was still going to see Dr Paviour and although he did his best to help, it was clear that the medication had largely worn off and that even the apomorphine drug was no longer effective.

I was confined to my bedroom most of the time, still exhausted by the pneumonia attack at Christmas. Dr Paviour was not as definite as Dr Milton in predicting the date of my expiry but he accepted that I was now very tired and said that another chest infection would finish me off.

Having been close to death once already, I viewed my impending demise quite dispassionately, indeed in an unemotional way that surprised even me. I found myself quite looking forward to it, if not the business of it but as the end of a life during which I had been ill for twenty-five per cent of the time and from which there was no other possibility of escape.

Death seemed ever more attractive after one particular freeze that had left me almost completely vitrified for ten hours. When I finally thawed at about 6.30 pm I suffered a severe bout of dyskinesia (shaking) which lasted for three hours. Feeling, indeed hoping, that this was the end, I took eight sleeping pills, four times the recommended amount. I got into bed and waited to sleep. Joyce got in beside me and we hugged and said goodbye, quite calmly now, because we both felt that enough was enough.

The next thing I knew it was 6.30 am. I woke, blinked, and remembered the excesses of the night before. I whispered an expletive under my breath. Then I paused for a moment as the early morning sunshine poured through the thin bedroom curtains.

I turned and looked at Joyce who was still sleeping soundly. Taking care not to disturb her, I slipped out of bed and sat in the chair beside it. I felt no ill effects from my excessive consumption of tablets the night before. Although I felt ambivalent about my situation at that moment, I had to admit that I felt glad to be alive.

This was followed quickly by a lurch into the abyss of depression as the reality of my illness struck me hard, as it had done every day for the last ten years. The day ahead was going to be a hell of a struggle but somehow I would get through it.

Against the odds my health began to improve in the late spring of 2016. During the summer, I regained some of my strength. It seemed possible that I might even make it to Christmas and confound Dr Milton's predictions.

Nevertheless, Joyce remained anxious and made her annual trip to see family in Hong Kong at my insistence, afraid that she might not see me again.

She must have given the matter a good deal of thought while she was away, because soon after her return she suddenly said one evening, 'I think I have done all I can do for you.' At first, I was alarmed by this, thinking she was about to abandon me, leaving me to face the end on my own.

I should have known better. What she meant was that physically and emotionally she was drained and that we needed to get some help.

Joyce undertook some research and found a care agency with a good reputation. They searched their files and identified someone who they felt matched our requirements.

The first carer was reasonably competent but the chemistry between us was not ideal.

We had far more luck with the second. Jola was a charming lady from Poland who made a big difference to our lives. The time came when Jola had to return to Poland to see her family and take some holiday. We were concerned about her temporary replacement but we need not have worried.

Ana, who Jola knew well, turned out to be a gem, a one in a million. Highly competent at everything she does, whether driving, cooking, gardening, making the TV work or fixing my recalcitrant personal computer, she has made an enormous difference to our lives and I hope she can be persuaded to stay for the rest of my life.

In July we also went to see Dr Paviour again, but this time he had an interesting proposal to put to us. He asked 'Would you like to be considered for Deep Brain Stimulation surgery (DBSS)?' This, of course, was what we had gone to talk to Alison Leake about two years previously.

Having been in St George's Hospital once already in recent months and subjected to one major procedure, I was not immediately keen to submit to a second in a year. I had read the reports of having holes drilled in your head while you were conscious. I also knew that DBSS was no guarantee of success and that there were inevitably some risks that it would make things worse. I asked myself if it were not simply delaying the inevitable.

I thought again, briefly, about going to Zurich or Basle in search of an easy and painless exit from what, for me, was a life which held little pleasure and which was dragging Joyce down too.

We asked around, unable to make what, at the time, was a very difficult choice.

Finally, Joyce wrote to a lifelong friend, the leading neurologist Bell Tse, in Hong Kong and sought his advice. He in turn consulted his niece, a neurologist in Mount Sinai Hospital, New York, who has more experience in DBSS. A few days later Bell came back to us with a view. He said he understood it was a very difficult decision, that there were risks in any surgery, but that if he were in my position he would say yes and give it a go. So that is what we did.

The build-up to DBSS was protracted and thorough.

First, I was given a full physical examination, ECG, more bloods and blood pressure tests, and then a full scan under general anaesthetic since I had developed a serious problem with claustrophobia.

Next came a test of memory and cognitive functions requiring six and a half hours, without respite, of relentless testing by the charming but ruthless Doctor Lucia Ricciardi. I passed the verbal test with flying colours, which gave me childish satisfaction. I went home exhausted that day, but so did Joyce who had been an observer.

The penultimate stage was a meeting with the team that was going to perform the operation. I was surprised by how many people were involved. It was about the size of a football team. Although Dr Paviour, a man of considerable distinction, chaired the group, it also included the acknowledged star, Professor Dr Francesca Morgante. She was a tiny woman with a winning smile, a Sicilian, who had recently joined the department and was widely regarded as one of the top neurologists in the world. The meeting, which I found reassuring and compassionate, was an opportunity for the team to weigh me up, to explain the procedures so that there would be no surprises and to set out the risks so that there could be no recriminations.

Mr Erlick Pereira, who was to perform the operation, said that if successful, I might expect a fifty per cent improvement, fifty per cent of the time.

Dr Paviour said that if he gave the green light they could schedule the surgery for the following February, at which point Joyce made one of her protective interventions, pointing out that we had been given a provisional date of November. She added that we would much prefer the earlier date rather than go through another winter and risk getting another chest infection. Doctor Paviour made a note and Joyce registered another victory over the NHS administration. The date was set for 29 November 2016.

There was one last pre operation check to ensure I was strong enough to undergo surgery: heart, blood pressure, and all the usual tests with which I had become so familiar. Then I was asked if I would like to see a psychiatrist.

'Why on earth would I want to do that,' I said?

'Because you say you sometimes get depressed,' they answered.

'Well,' I replied, 'it's like this, if you could not stand, walk, swallow, sleep, or move at all for several hours at a time how would you feel? A bit miffed, perhaps?'

The proposal was dropped.

I think I must have been so desperate by then that the prospect of someone drilling holes in my head while I was wide awake held no fear, and I felt entirely relaxed when we checked in the night before.

After the horrors of the Marnham Ward I was pleasantly surprised and pleased to be given a private room on a neurological ward and I thanked Mr Pereira who came to see me that evening.

He asked me how I was feeling and I said fine and that I had no fear because I had absolute faith in his ability. 'But,' I

278

said, 'if you do make a mistake, please make sure it is a big one. I have no wish to become a vegetable.'

He smiled and said he was sure it would go well.

I asked him how many of these operations he had performed and he said more than 100. That sounded good but I lacked the courage to ask what success rate he had achieved.

As instructed, I stopped taking all medication from that point on, went to bed cold turkey and slept for a dreamless six hours.

They came for me in the morning all prepared for an early start. One of the porters recognised me from my stay at the hospital twelve months previously. 'Nice to see you again, sir,' he said 'you'll be fine; a strong man like you will have no trouble.'

I thanked him for his reassurance.

They took me into a room where the doctors prepare themselves and the patients are made ready for surgery. Mr Pereira was ready and waiting. He greeted me warmly from behind his surgical mask. Under his direction the porters then slid me from the bed onto a flat trolley. He began to attach some sort of steel contraption onto my head but all I could see was a type of visor in front of my nose and mouth. It gripped my head with four steel pins and together with the band running across my face the visor immobilised my head completely. He sprayed on a local anaesthetic and then

279

tightened each of the four steel pins until they punctured my skin and caused quite a lot of bleeding as head wounds always do and he wiped it away.

It hurt a good deal but to prove to myself and to convince him of my resolve, I made a point of not making a sound.

'Well done,' he said, 'I know that isn't pleasant but believe it or not that's probably the worst part over already. We should be ready to start soon.'

I heard him leave the room then come back a few minutes later. 'We are all here,' he said, 'but there is a bit of a problem. They forgot to switch the heating on. It may take a couple of hours until the theatre reaches the temperature at which we can operate safely. What would you say if we remove the frame, take you back to your room and then come back here tomorrow?'

'No bloody way,' I said, 'I haven't built myself up for this day to see nothing happen. It is not fair to me and grossly unfair to my wife who is waiting at home in a state of anxiety. She and our carer will come to the hospital a bit later expecting a result.'

'Fully understood,' said Mr Pereira and left the room to confer with colleagues.

He came back a few minutes later. 'If you can tolerate having your head held in a vice for three hours instead of one, we will go ahead as soon as the room is ready.'

'So be it,' I said, 'I will wait and I promise not to wander off; I don't think I look my best in this headgear.'

He chortled and patted me on the shoulder. 'Well done you,' he said, 'that's the spirit.'

I was left on the table for almost two hours, my head held in the vice-like grip of the steel guard and staring at the ceiling because it wasn't possible to stare anywhere else.

After an hour my lower back began to hurt – an old rugby injury – and I was just beginning to doubt the wisdom of my decision to tough it out when a nurse came to check on me and realised that I was getting cold. Quickly she covered me with one of those special blankets they use to revive victims of hypothermia.

Eventually, Mr Pereira came back, and apologised profusely for something he and his colleagues had every right to be angry about.

Finally, Dr Paviour, Dr Morgante and Dr Ricciardi took me into the operating theatre where I was greeted enthusiastically. However, from then on Mr Pereira was clearly in charge of the whole process, which followed a well-rehearsed pattern as he snapped out the instructions. Everyone did exactly what they were told.

A spot of local anaesthetic on the side of my head was followed by the touch of something cold and hard. Suddenly I heard the start of an electric drill and felt it touch my head. There was no pain but I found the sound of the drilling so close to my ear a little disturbing.

'This is not much worse than a trip to the dentist, is it?' said Mr Pereira. By then he had finished off the hole he had made with a manual drill. That made a sound that I had not heard since woodwork classes at Sedbergh and the image that came to mind was not pleasing.

Mr Pereira finished one side of my head and then turned his attention to the other, repeating the process.

When both were finished, the complex business began of inserting the stimulators. This demanded a good deal of cooperation between Dr Morgante who was sitting behind me (presumably looking at a camera inside my head) and giving guidance to Dr Paviour who stood in front of me. She kept asking me to recite things such as the months of the year, the days of the week, the letters of the alphabet, then repeating them in reverse order, and then nursery rhymes as they moved the stimulators around to find the optimum position. I heard a massive improvement in my speech as they did so which I found very exciting. The positioning of the stimulators is all-important. It has to be absolutely precise if they are to be fully effective, so this process took a good deal of time until they were satisfied. Eventually they agreed that they were correctly positioned, plugged the holes and sewed them up.

They then went into a prolonged huddle on the other side of the room while I remained stretched out on the operating table. My head did not hurt at all but my lower back ached badly from having no support and for two hours more than originally planned.

At long last they came out of their huddle. To my profound relief Mr Pereira released me from the steel vice and I was able to move my head and shoulders again relatively easily and to relieve the painful pressure on my back.

After about twenty minutes, they took me to another part of the theatre and, after some encouraging remarks about how it was going, the anaesthetist put me to sleep for an hour or so for the second part of the operation.

This consisted of inserting a battery in my chest and attaching it to the stimulators by a wire running up the inside of my neck. To this day I have no idea exactly how this feat was achieved.

When I came to, after the whole operation was over, I was in the recovery room. I opened my eyes to find most of the team standing round the bed looking down on me benevolently as though I were a newborn baby.

Dr Morgante spoke for the team. She said, 'Well done Michael. I am so proud of you.' (I didn't ask why, I hadn't done anything; I had been unconscious for the last hour and a half).

Mr Pereira opined that it was one of the best three such operations he had ever performed. He said, 'You were great.'

I was taken back to the ward feeling pleased with myself and was met by a jubilant Joyce and Ana who had been told the good news.

Together, we drafted an email to all my friends who had taken an active interest and Joyce sent it out the same evening.

'Dear friends and family,

As you probably know Mike underwent Deep Brain Stimulation surgery today. The six-hour operation was performed by a team at St George's Hospital in London. It was the latest and probably the last step in his twelve-year battle with Parkinson's Disease. There is no cure for PD and it will be several weeks before the success of the DBSS can be fully assessed when the electrodes are activated.

However, the hospital reports that the operation, albeit gruelling, was a great success. Mike's neurosurgeon and neurologists are confident that it will result in a significant reduction in his symptoms and that he will enjoy a much better quality of life.

Mike is in good spirits. True to form he has said that his top priority is to go home as soon as possible and to check that neither the electrodes inserted in his brain nor the battery implanted in his chest interfere with TV reception of the England v Australia rugby match on Saturday.

I am immensely proud of the courage with which Mike has faced his long ordeal of a terrible illness, and we are deeply thankful for the skill and dedication of the doctors and nurses of the Atkinson Morley Wing of St George's. But most of all we are profoundly grateful for the love, encouragement and unwavering support of family and friends. From the bottom of our hearts we thank you.'

I stayed in hospital for another two days and was feeling well and anxious to get home.

Dr Paviour came by and on the second occasion he brought with him what looked like an ordinary laptop but with some sort of connected electronic device, which he placed in my top pocket. He turned his laptop on. He ran through the system and carried out some tests, after which he assured me that everything was working exactly as it should. He warned me that I would feel no immediate benefit. He asked me to go back in a week's time when he said they would turn the stimulators up.

Then I went home for the weekend as planned, feeling tired but keen to see what would happen when the system was switched on properly and optimistic that it would work.

Incredibly, I was joined that weekend by Anthony Rademeyer. He had flown all the way from his home in New Mexico (about twenty-two hours) just to sit with me for two days and to keep me company while I recuperated. As a single act of pure kindness and selfless friendship, I have never seen it surpassed...

The following Thursday, Joyce, Ana and I went back to St George's for my 'turning on' appointment. By coincidence we met Dr Morgante, Dr Ricciardi and Alison on the way in. As we all got into the lift together, they were laughing and smiling and exceptionally warm towards us. There appeared to be an air of celebration at the success of the operation and of my insistence on going ahead with it despite the setback of the unheated operating theatre.

Then we were all assembled in the room with me in a chair at one end of it, and most of the others seated at the other.

With the support of Dr Morgante, who whispered advice to him from time to time, Dr Paviour put the device he had used previously in my top pocket and turned on his laptop, tapping vigorously for a couple of minutes while Dr Morgante looked at me encouragingly.

'Stand up, would you?' said Dr Paviour.

I looked at him somewhat dubiously because I had not stood up for several weeks. But suddenly I felt a surge of power running through my body and into my legs. I stood up quite easily.

'Now walk,' he said and I, who had not walked in months, walked quite easily up and down the room.

'Now turn around,' said Dr Morgante, standing up and taking my hand and I did so a couple of times before sitting down again. The look of triumph was on everyone's faces but the smile on Joyce's face was the best thing I had seen in twenty years.

The next week I took the District Line to High Street Kensington. I crossed the busy street and walked through the gates into Kensington Gardens. Then I walked round the entire perimeter of the Gardens and Hyde Park. Just because I could.

Chapter 11 - Epilogue

'La lutte elle-même vers les sommets suffit à remplir un coeur
d'homme. Il faut imaginer Sysyphe heureux.'
('The struggle itself towards the summit is enough to fill a
man's heart. One must imagine Sisyphus is happy.')
Albert Camus, *The Myth of Sisyphus*

My excursion to Kensington would have made a good
end to this account of my life; it is optimistic, like the ending of
a Victorian novel.

Sadly, Parkinson's Disease is no respecter of literary
convention and my story does not end there. Although DBSS
was a great success, its influence wore off after a few months
even though Dr Paviour and Dr Morgante have adjusted the
stimulators again and again.

I now spend most of my time in a wheelchair. Things
can only get worse. I do not know how much longer I will last
and my sole preoccupation now is to leave Joyce in as good a
position as possible when the inevitable happens.

And that is almost the end of my story. However, as I
was putting the finishing touches to the text, some new and
interesting information came to light. I had based my account
of the background on three long meetings with Catherine and

on our voluminous correspondence. Her memory was obviously good, her recollections vivid and I had no reason to doubt that she was telling the truth. Or at least that she believed she was. She always maintained that she could tell me next to nothing about the life of Fred (Jack) prior to their first meeting because he would never talk about it. I found this gap frustrating but I was so preoccupied with the physical difficulty of writing that I lacked the wits or the energy to set about trying to fill it. In particular, I wanted to confirm where Fred came from and when and where he died. It would make for a tidy conclusion. Catherine had told me that he was buried at Peaslake in Surrey but when Joyce and I went there on a grey day one January, we searched the small cemetery for forty-five minutes, sweeping the snow off some of the flat headstones, and found nothing. Later I mentioned this to some friends to whom I am deeply indebted. Intelligent and resourceful as they are, they started to dig and quite quickly produced some information that had eluded even Ariel Bruce. A surprising and relevant picture emerged.

Fred (not 'Frederick') was born in March 1896, not in Ireland as Catherine had surmised, but in nearby Eaton Bray, a tiny village in Bedfordshire. He was the first son of Frederick Arthur Tooley and Maria Tooley (née Pratt). Mr Tooley was the owner of a mill. In the course of the next ten years he and his wife had five more children, four daughters and a second son, Frank. You might form a picture of a prosperous and happy family and so it may have been except for one important change. The 1901 census forms show that Fred, aged five, was no longer living with his parents and younger brother and sisters but with his maternal grandparents who were farmers in the next village of Edlesborough. You can imagine the effect on Fred of having to look back at the house where his mother and siblings still lived but from which he was banished.

A 1911 census form shows Fred's family at Eaton Bray Mills but there is no record of the fifteen-year-old Fred, who had left home possibly intending to join the army as soon as he could.

The next time he comes into focus is during the Great War when, in the defining moments of his life 'Mad Jack' Tooley wins two military crosses in less than a year.

His father died in 1935, a wealthy man, but Fred was not named as a beneficiary. His mother died two years later leaving only a modest estate but including both Fred and Frank as beneficiaries.

There was little sign of a reconciliation by the end of the Great War. Fred, by now a highly decorated officer, married Dorothy Weitzel at St Michael's Parish Church, Golder's Green in 1918. His mother signed the register but not his father who, despite his son's acknowledged heroism, presumably did not attend the wedding.

Now comes the big surprise. I had asked Catherine if Fred and Dorothy had produced any children during their twenty-year marriage; she said they had not. She was most definite on this point. However, there is clear evidence that Dorothy gave birth to two sons, Peter and David and a daughter, Molly. Sometime after 1939 it seems that Fred walked out on the marriage leaving his wife and children, never to return. Rejection and separation again. He broke all ties with his past and by the end of the Second World War he was just plain Jack Tooley, bon viveur, wit, ex-soldier, and friend to all the world. You wonder how much the man who limped into Catherine's life in 1945 was damaged by war and how much by childhood rejection.

Once I discovered that I had half-siblings, I made contact with David's son, Frank and learnt that apart from him, David also had another son, Andy and two daughters, Frances and Angela. Peter had one daughter, Rachael.

Sadly, Peter, David and Molly have died.

I have since met with Frank and Rachael, who are both warm and kind and bear a striking resemblance to me. Although we are all similar in age, I am proud to be their half-uncle.

Catherine died a year ago last January, although I do not know the exact date. The letter from the solicitor in Bradford-on-Avon was strangely imprecise, referring to 'the recent passing of Mrs Tooley' as though I knew about it already. I didn't. She was a few months short of 100 years old.

The solicitor called me a few days after her death to tell me that she had left a will but that I was not a beneficiary. This surprised me a little, because Ariel Bruce had said that Catherine had made a will in my favour almost immediately after Ariel had contacted her for the first time. I suspect that her estate was very small. Even so, it would have been nice if she had left me something, such as Jack's medals. She knew I was interested in military history. The solicitor said, 'By the way, are you the son?'

'Yes,' I said. And that was all I said.

'Thank you,' he said and put the phone down.

I felt a slight sense of rejection, and then dismissed it. There was too much else going on.

Jack died on 28 May 1964, a broken old man of 68. Catherine would not talk about the period immediately after his death, except to say that, 'It had been difficult.' She lived on her own for the next 53 years. Eventually, in middle age, she found work more suited to her ability. She became the bursar of a prominent school in Wimbledon and, having worked there for a few years, she became the practice manager of a GP's surgery in Sutton. She never bought a house or a flat, which she said she regretted ('There was always a new dress or a new pair of shoes I wanted'). By the time I first met her she was living in a modest but spotlessly clean apartment a short walk from the surgery from which she had retired five years earlier. She was already talking of moving to somewhere bigger in a more peaceful area.

By the time of our next meeting, she was living in semi-sheltered accommodation in Bradford-on-Avon. We had a walk around the town and I judged it a far more pleasant place than Sutton. However, our conversation had become stilted again and I was relieved to get away, glad that she was comfortable and in a place where she said she had friends. I felt no other obligation to her.

It is hard to describe to a fit person what it is like to have an incurable illness. In the case of Parkinson's Disease, every case is different. However, the common or garden strain, which I have, is best understood through a metaphor. If a heart attack is a cobra strike, Parkinson's is a python that coils itself around its victim and gradually tightens its hold, squeezing the life out of them. Or, if you prefer a more commonplace image, think of one of those machines they use in hospital to measure blood pressure. They put an inflatable band around your upper arm and then pump it until it is tight and starts to hurt. Having PD is like having not just your arm, but your entire body, inside one of those bands. And it keeps squeezing.

In order to survive long-term illness, you need three things; first, the best medical care you can get or afford; secondly, supportive family and friends; and thirdly, an iron will. When I said this to my brother-in-law Lawrence, who has been chief executive of the two leading university hospitals in Hong Kong, he said that I was spot on except that I should reverse the order.

I have come to the conclusion that assisted suicide should be made legal and more readily available, although strictly controlled and properly supervised. I recognise that there is a very big difference between euthanasia and making the choice to die. Nevertheless, in the course of my life I have taken seven pets to the vet's to be 'put to sleep.' On each occasion I have been heart broken but the overwhelming sensation is one of relief – relief that the animal's suffering has come to an end gently and peacefully. I have felt no guilt but on occasion have reproached myself for not acting sooner. If we can do this great service to our animals, why not for ourselves? I know precisely what lies ahead for me if my condition is allowed to run its full course. I do not fear death. I do find the prospect of dying in such circumstances with the loss of human dignity it involves intolerable. I have resolved not to allow it to happen. I hope I have shown enough resilience over the last fifteen years for those who know me not to doubt my courage.

I used to think that the most valuable human attribute was intelligence. I was wrong. I still have respect for intellect but I now believe that by far the greatest attribute is kindness. The best of mankind has both intellect and compassion.

Once upon a time, when Rousseau was one of the most influential thinkers in Europe, it was believed that mankind as a species could improve through a creative engagement with nature. By the end of the Great War, that notion was dying and, by the end of the Second World War, it was extinguished. As an American poet said, 'Man has not been himself since God died'. However, I believe that most people, in the right conditions, will behave decently.

Our generation, at least in Western Europe, has been the most fortunate in human history. We have had no wars to fight; we live longer, healthier lives. Materially we are better off than our parents, we have more leisure time, more disposable income, bigger pensions, more travel, more entertainment *and* we own property. The next generation may find life altogether more difficult.

I respect absolutely anyone's right to believe in God and to worship in any way they feel. I was brought up in a deeply Christian family and I believe I have Christian values. However, belief in God ultimately requires a leap of faith. It is hard to make that leap when you are sitting in a wheelchair. I am not alone in finding death, disease, and untold suffering hard to reconcile with the concept of God. I see little sign of the devil either although a few humans are pure evil. I do not feel a victim of some malign force, merely an example of what Darwin called nature's 'random cruelty.' As for the appropriate response to the eternal question, 'What does it all mean?' the only thing that occurs to me is a last act of defiance at the absurdity of it all; it is laughter.

London, May 2018

The Water's Edge

I have died.

I have walked up to the water's edge,

And felt death's touch on my toes.

I have travelled near enough

To feel your breath on my cheeks,

To know again how it is to be loved,

To be the most important person to someone

Who died

But is still alive in me

Still.

I have died

To hold you alive in my heart.

I have missed you so,

My love.

My life review of our time together,

I watch more closely

Your every flaw, your intention, intelligence, wit.

Your love for me

For others.

You cried with me, talked about your hurt, your fears,
your desires, dreams.
In a flash, they slip through your fingers.

I hold you still
In my death,
Sprinkled with the waves at the water's edge.

You are mine,
Still mine.
Unlost,
Remembered.

Joyce Chiu Broadbent, April 2019

Explanation of Terms/Glossary

Chapter 1

'swell a progress' – from *The Love Song of J. Alfred Prufrock* (1917)

Chapter 2

'This Jack spent a year in Changi and two years on the Burma railway as a guest of the Japanese.' – He was held in Changi prison in Singapore and was one of the prisoners of war subjected to forced labour on the Burma railway, which was also known as the Death Railway.

Chapter 8

The Princely Hong was a nickname for Jardine Matheson. (Hong means merchant/company in Chinese.) James Clavell wrote a 1996 bestseller called *Tai Pan* (which means ruler in Chinese) about the boss of a powerful Hong Kong trading company. Some said the book was about Jardine Matheson.

Gweilo – an affectionate term for white people, which can be translated as ghost man

PPE - Philosophy, politics and economics or politics, philosophy, and economics (PPE) is an interdisciplinary undergraduate or postgraduate degree which combines study from three disciplines. The first institution to offer degrees in PPE was the University of Oxford in the 1920s.